ABANDONED BUT NOT ALONE

My quest to find the mother who gave me away

John Lomacang

Pacific Press® Publishing Association
Nampa, Idaho
Oshawa, Ontario, Canada
www.pacificpress.com

Edited by Jerry D. Thomas
Cover Design by Dennis Ferree
Cover Photo, Steve Welsh Studios; Inset supplied by the author
Inside Design by Steve Lanto

Copyright © 2002 by
Pacific Press® Publishing Association
Printed in the United States of America
All Rights Reserved

Additional copies of this book may be purchased at
http://www.adventistbookcenter.com

ISBN 0-8163-1914-6

05 06 • 5 4 3

Contents

1. If He Only Knew 7
2. But Not Forgotten 16
3. My Anchors 26
4. "How Did You Know?" 35
5. God and His Lovely Assistant 45
6. A New Beginning . . . Together 55
7. Taking Off 64
8. More Than Wonderful 74
9. Look Out, World—Here We Come! 99
10. The Power of Faith 109
11. Starting Over 116
12. My Biological Mother 128
13. Not Enough Time 134
14. Precious Papa 139
15. Dreams Come True 144
Appendix 150

A poet can take a worthless sheet of paper, write a poem on it, and make it worth $3,000; that's genius. A businessman can sign his name on a piece of paper and make it worth a million dollars; that is prosperity. Your country's treasurer can take metal, stamp an emblem on it, and make it worth a dollar; that is money. A tradesman can take five dollars worth of metal and make it into something worth twenty-five dollars; that is skill. An artist can take a piece of canvas, paint a picture on it, and make it worth $5,000; that is art. But only God can take a worthless, sinful life, wash it in the blood of Jesus, put His Holy Spirit in it, and make it a blessing to humanity; that is a miracle.

" 'Can a woman forget her nursing child, and not have compassion on the son of her womb? Surely they may forget, yet I will not forget you' " (Isaiah 49:15, NKJV).

CHAPTER ONE

If He Only Knew

As the rising October sun painted the skyline of a crisp New York morning, Rosie wiped her eyes. She turned slowly from the frosted window, unable to escape the decision she had made. Only the hissing steam that pushed its way through the radiator broke the silence in her small, dimly lighted apartment. After a vigorous rub of her upper arms in an attempt to dispel the cold, she placed her hand softly on the brow of her three-month-old baby boy, John. Through her tears and quivering lips, she slowly whispered, "I'm doing this only because I love you. Please understand, please."

Rosie's silent weeping was interrupted by the gentle tug and soft voice of her three-year-old daughter, Vivian. "Mommy, what's the matter? Are you OK?"

Rosie brushed away her tears. "I'm OK, Val. Mommy will be right there to help you get dressed. Don't forget, we have to get ready to go to Momma Haynes's real soon." Rosie always called Vivian "Val."

Momma Haynes was the baby sitter. For three months she had cared for Rosie's children, and she had grown genuinely fond of them. Through mutual acquaintances, Rosie had heard of this lady that many just referred to as "Momma Haynes." If ever there was a woman that knew how to share love, she was the one. If compassion and tenderness had a face, it would have to be hers.

Rosie walked to the window again, and this time, instead of just looking through the glass, she slowly opened the window, knelt down, and leaned forward on the ledge. The clicking heels of rushing pedestrians, the rumbling undertones of the passing subway trains, and the reverberating sound of a cab's horn all too clearly reminded her that *the day* had come.

After that frozen moment, Rosie quickly rose to her feet and got back on her schedule. Grabbing her small hard-shell blue-and-white travel case, she walked to the dresser drawer and began folding John's baby clothes one at a time and placing them into the silk-lined case. Each tiny garment brought more tears. Gathering Val's clothes took only a moment more. Quickly, she and the children were ready to leave.

This day would begin with a journey that would last for almost twenty-six years.

With skill only a mother can appreciate, Rosie backed out of the apartment and locked the door with one hand while balancing her bags, her pocketbook, and her infant son with the other. Then she turned quickly and began her slow but careful descent down the two flights of stairs that seemed to wind endlessly through the cold hallways of this Manhattan tenement.

With John tucked securely in his blue blanket close to her chest and Val by the hand, Rosie made her way down the steps and down the street. For some reason the subway seemed farther than usual. Everything seemed to slow down. It was like being trapped in a movie scene that refused to end. To Rosie, even the people walking on the streets seemed to be crossing her path in an attempt to avert the inevitable. She shook her head. *I've got to do this! It's too late to turn back now!*

Every step made the next one easier. With every breath, the five-foot frame of this petite woman carried her to an appointment with destiny.

After a final rush to purchase a token as the train clattered into the station, Rosie took the seat offered to her by a kind gentleman and sighed with relief. With baby John asleep on her right arm and Val on her lap, she had nothing to do but think. The battle of her heart and mind raged fiercely. The questions seemed to be louder than the answers. *Am I doing the right thing? What will Mrs. Haynes think of me? Would things be different if Johnny and I had stayed together? How did I get myself in this mess, anyway? Is it too late to change my mind?*

Johnny was a musician that Rosie met and dated for a short time. He was the father of her baby John. They fell in and out of love. They were together just long enough to give John life.

The train conductor's voice broke through the storm in Rosie's mind. "Franklin Avenue next stop!"

Rosie placed a soft kiss on Val's forehead. "Wake up, honey; our stop is next."

Standing at the top of the steps at the Franklin Avenue train station, Rosie stared at the street before her. The pharmacy and Mr. Lee's Chinese restaurant were on her left. One block in the distance stood Public School #3. *Could that be the school that my children will attend one day?* she wondered.

She walked down Franklin Avenue, crossing Putnam, then down one more street to reach Madison Street. The familiar walk seemed longer and more difficult this time. Val broke the painful silence by pointing to the house and exclaiming, "There it is, Mommy." The baby sitter's house stood in the shadows of the Nativity Catholic School and the church. As Rosie approached Mrs. Haynes's gate, the uniformed school children were hurrying to school.

As was her custom, Mrs. Haynes was waiting by her window. With the blinds open, she could be ready to greet the children and their parents. She hurried to the gate. "Good morning, Rosario!"

"Good morning, Momma Haynes. Here are your favorite children." Mrs. Haynes was everyone's "mom." Maybe her love for children was so intense because she never had natural children of her own. This desire to love was not wasted. Instead of lamenting her fate, Momma Haynes shared her love with every parent and child who came to her home.

Mrs. Haynes, formerly Carmen Pyle, was born and raised in the West Indian country of Trinidad. Her father passed away when she was young, but her mother, Nina, lovingly cared for her. It was in Port of Spain, Trinidad, where she met her husband, George.

George was from Barbados. He had lost both of his parents when he was young. He and his three younger brothers were raised by their grandmother in Christ Church, Barbados.

Carmen was a schoolteacher at the time when George came to Trinidad from Barbados to seek work. He accepted a job painting the school where Carmen was teaching. On one very humid day, Carmen noticed him perched on a ladder outside her classroom. Taking a short break from her students, she went out and offered him a glass of cold water. "From the looks of how hard you are working, you need a drink," she said.

George paused and wiped his face with the small cloth that he had on his shoulders. "Thanks! I'm determined to finish this small area, so I haven't stopped to get water." As he reached for the water, his eyes met hers. The painting job lasted only four weeks, but it was long enough for them to talk each day. It was long enough for him to know that he would stay in Trinidad longer than he had planned.

George and Carmen were married in 1938, and ten years later, they moved to Brooklyn, New York. Before they left Trinidad, they found a little boy named Kelvin wandering the streets. His parents were too poor to raise him, so they gave him to Mr. and Mrs. Haynes. They adopted Kelvin and brought him to America, where he lived for the remainder of his life.

Rosie had heard this story more than once. As she handed over her baby, she could see the love in Momma Haynes's eyes. "Rosario, how's he doing today? Have you taken him to the clinic to see what's wrong with him?"

"The doctor just told me that he needs good nourishment," Rosie replied. "I have this prescription for vitamins to put in his milk."

Little Val stood between her mother and Momma Haynes, looking back and forth at them. Val didn't like being left at the baby sitter's, but

Momma Haynes had a gift for making Val comfortable. Each day the routine was the same. Val would cry for a short time after her mother left, and John would just sleep.

Momma Haynes looked at the extra clothes and things Rosie had with her. "Rosario, why did you bring so much today?"

Rosie swallowed as she quickly thought up an explanation. "I decided to give you more clothes so I would not have to bring any with me each day. This way I could make changes at the end of the week rather than every day."

Momma Haynes nodded slowly. "Well, all right. I guess that makes sense."

Rosie went on. "I have some extra baby bottles too. They're in the shoulder bag, wrapped in his diapers. And just in case John wakes in the night, there are some extra pacifiers for him. He sleeps well if he has one."

Momma Haynes turned and looked at Rosie. "What do you mean by *night*? Aren't you coming back later to pick them up?"

Rosie quickly realized that she had made a mistake. "What I meant was, when he sleeps at night, I give him a pacifier. I guess it could also work for him while he sleeps in the day." She nervously looked away so that Momma Haynes would not see her eyes. Then she gestured as if she was looking at her watch. "Well, I have to go. I don't want to be late."

Then she knelt down and called, "Val, come give Mommy a hug." As Val ran into her arms, the phone rang, distracting Mrs. Haynes. Rosie took the opportunity to say Goodbye to her little girl. With tears welling up in her eyes, the words came out slowly. "Remember, Mommy loves you, very much. Don't ever forget that. Tell your baby brother that I love him very much, OK?"

Val looked intently into her mother's eyes as if she was recording every word. With one final kiss, Rosie said, "Mommy loves you." Then she walked to the crib where John was resting and leaned forward to kiss him on his tender face. A tear fell to his cheek. As she reached forward to wipe it away, she whispered, "Mommy loves you."

As Momma Haynes returned, Rosie wiped her eyes and said, "Take good care of them for me."

Without realizing the full impact of her words, Momma Haynes replied, "You know I love them as if they were my own. You can count on it."

With a final "Thanks so much," Rosie turned and began her slow, empty journey into a new life. This time the streets were silent. This time her arms were empty—no son to cradle, no daughter to lead. This journey would prove to be the most difficult of her life.

What would bring a young mother to this difficult intersection of life? What would push her to make such a life-wrenching decision? How could she walk away from two innocent and fragile lives?

Back on the subway, Rosie reached into her pocket and pulled out a small, neatly folded piece of paper. The night before, as she wrestled with the decision to leave her children, John was particularly on her mind. She had written out her pact with the Lord. The note said: "Lord, I'm giving you my son and my daughter. Take care of them for me. Lord, especially look out for John—he's not too well. I'm giving him to You—just give him back to me one day."

Back at her apartment, Rosie looked at the dresser drawer that doubled as John's crib. She looked at Val's little cot that lay close to her bed. Everywhere she looked was a memory too great to silence. Rosie walked over to her bed and leaned back on the pillow. Before long she was fast asleep.

George Haynes arrived home from work that evening to find his wife, Carmen, sitting in the kitchen trying to calm Rosie's daughter, Val. Through her little tears, Val kept repeating, "I want my Mommy."

"Where's Rosario?" George asked.

Carmen shook her head. "I thought she would be here by now. She's never been this late before."

"Did you call her job?" George asked.

"Yes I did, but they said she didn't come to work today. I also called her at home, but there was no answer. Maybe something happened to her. What should we do?"

George sat at the table with Carmen, and they both looked at each other as if to be searching for answers. Val sat in a chair nearby, while John played with a rattle in his crib. Finally, Carmen said, "This is *not* like Rosario. If she were going to be late, she would call and let me know something." George urged Carmen to call Rosie's home again. By now it was nearing 10:00 p.m.

Rosie was sitting on her bed in the dark room when the phone rang. She didn't move. Without a doubt, she knew that the baby sitter was calling. Her swollen, red eyes didn't look up from the empty box of tissues beside her. The phone rang about fifteen times, but she could only whisper, "Please stop ringing."

After hanging up, the Hayneses called the police. When a patrol car arrived at almost 11:30 p.m., the bewildered couple greeted the officers and answered all the questions they could. When the officers saw that both Val and John had fallen asleep, they suggested that the children stay there for the night. "We'll make some inquiries and be in touch in the morning."

Rosie had thought her plan through pretty thoroughly. *If I am going to stay hidden, I need to make some drastic changes quickly.* She knew that people would be looking for her. She arranged to stay with a friend for a few weeks and quit her job.

From day to day, the officers kept searching. From day to day, they kept the Hayneses informed. But New York is a big city, and if you want to hide, you can stay hidden. After a specified length of time had passed, the laws of the city allowed Mr. and Mrs. Haynes to be awarded custody of the abandoned children.

Rosie had determined that this couple was well-equipped financially and socially to raise her children. She also knew that Momma Haynes had a particular love for her children. When baby John had to return to the hospital for surgery to repair a hernia, Momma Haynes had visited him each day and taken him to her home as he recovered.

Rosie's deep love for John and Val led her to the best place to leave them. This was not the first time Rosie had left a child behind.

So much had happened to Rosie in just the last six years. For whatever reason, she wasn't pleased with her life. She was fond of her children, but with all the other choices that she made, they just didn't seem to fit into her plans. In 1952, just 19 years old, Rosie had a son named James. She called him Jimmy. He, too, was born in New York; but eight months later, Rosie took him back to her home—in St. Thomas, US Virgin Islands.

When Rosie arrived home, she gave Jimmy to her sister Theresa Maria to look after for her. Theresa's husband was in the navy, on Roosevelt Island Naval Base, in Puerto Rico, so they took Jimmy there with them. After almost a year, Rosie brought her son back to St. Thomas. When Rosie showed up at her mother's house with Jimmy in her arms, her mother was startled. "What do you plan to do with a child when you're so young?"

Rosie looked at her mother's husband, Andre, and announced, "Here is the son you always wanted." She gave Jimmy to her mother, Inger, and Andre to keep for a short while.

Rosie stayed on the island until 1954. She dated a musician named Harry Lang for a short while. They were together long enough to conceive. Pregnant with her second child, Rosie left St. Thomas and returned to New York City. Vivian (Val) was born in May 1955.

Rosie occasionally took little Val with her as she visited some of the nightspots of New York. One evening when Val was about two, they sat at a table in a small club and listened to John Parker play his horn. He must have noticed the attractive, stylishly dressed woman. John Parker recalls that when he met Rosie, she told him that her name was Kim. This was another way Rosie remained anonymous. This way she could move in and out of situations and cover her tracks. After two failed relationships, Rosie had learned how to disappear as needed. After her last child—John—was born, her relationship with John Parker began to fall apart.

If Rosie didn't want you to find her, you couldn't. When she decided to close a door, it remained closed until she decided to open it. When she decided to end a relationship, it remained that way.

Rosie was a good seamstress. Her mother had taught both Rosie and her sister, Theresa, how to sew. Due to her resourcefulness, Rosie was somehow able to survive on her own. A carefree spirit, she could talk her way into and out of almost any situation. She was determined to make life what she pictured it should be.

By the fall of 1958, her desperate attempt to design her life had left her with three children and nothing to call her own. She was not even caring for her children. As sad as this was, Rosie made these decisions. No one forced her hand. She had such an unrealistic view of life that each day was an attempt to make the next day better. Possibly the lack of a father as she grew up affected her view of love. Perhaps it was her quest to replace that love that sent her "looking for love in all the wrong places."

The irony of her life is that even though she could not find love, one day love would find her.

Meanwhile, back at the Hayneses, Val sensed that something was terribly wrong. When Rosie had not returned in days, Val became reclusive and, for a time, untrusting. Even as young as John was, he must have missed his mother's touch and her smile. Perhaps in his own peculiar way, baby John knew that his mother was gone.

What would he have said had he known? What would he have done? If he only knew, what difference would it have made to his outlook on life?

It would be some time before he would find out, but inevitably the day would come.

CHAPTER TWO

But Not Forgotten

Rosie remained in New York about eight more years after she left Val and me at the baby sitter's. Not too long after John Parker and Rosie (Kim, as he knew her to be) went their separate ways, Rosie went into survival mode. She moved, changed jobs, and used another name for a time. Meanwhile, she continued her quest for the ideal life. Her plan was to find the "right man," marry him, settle down—then go back for her three children. But her life took one unpredictable turn after another.

Rosie enjoyed shopping at the ritzy stores of New York. Looking good was a specialty that she painstakingly maintained. One afternoon she was having lunch in a quaint café off Fifth Avenue, in Manhattan, when a well-dressed gentleman walked over and introduced himself.

"My name is Jim Miller. Do you mind if I share your table with you?"

It was the beginning of a significant relationship. Over the next few months, Rosie and Jim saw each other frequently. He showered her with gifts and took her out on the town and away for long weekends. After about seven months, she moved into his apartment on the upper east side of Manhattan. They were together for seven years.

Rosie talked gladly about her three children, hoping that Jim would ask her to marry him and that they would raise her children together.

But Rosie's dream of "the perfect family" was shattered when she told Jim that her children were racially mixed. In the late 50s and early 60s, there was still a great divide about class distinction and the race barrier, even in the great diverse city of New York. Jim wasn't interested in placing himself in a situation that would increase the misunderstood and misplaced tensions of that era. Rosie decided to leave well enough alone. After all, her children were safe.

Through the years, Rosie would periodically send cards to her family in St. Thomas. Sometimes the cards had a return address and sometimes they didn't. At times the cards and letters were filled with the details of her experiences. Sometimes it would only be a card with four scribbled words: "Things are fine. Rosie."

On July 4, in 1964, the doorbell rang. When she went downstairs to answer it, Rosie saw a yellow envelope wedged between the door and the frame—a telegram. Ripping it open, she read, "Inger was killed in an accident. The wall that Andrea was building fell on her. She died instantly. Come home as soon as possible."

Rosie ran up the stairs and told Jim that she had to leave immediately. "What happened? Who was at the door? What's going on?" he asked. Rosie gave him the telegram to read, while she sat on the couch crying and softly repeating the words, "My mother's dead. My mother is dead."

Jim consoled her. "When do you have to leave?" he asked.

"Today!" They rushed to the airport, and Rosie was able to get aboard a flight that afternoon. When she arrived at the airport in St. Thomas, she asked, "How's Jimmy?"

"He's pretty broken up over the whole thing," her sister answered. "He still doesn't know that you are his mother. Mommy and Andre told him you are his sister."

Rosie was flabbergasted. "You mean to tell me that for the last nine years Jimmy has believed that I am his sister, not his mother?"

It was true. Rosie waited until after the funeral to tell him; but she knew it was time that Jimmy knew the truth. So at eleven years old, Jimmy was told for the first time that Rosie was his mother. It was too much for him to handle. The pain and disappointment of deception took its toll. Rosie remained in St. Thomas for two or three years, but she had a hard time convincing Jimmy that things could be different. Finally, she decided that it would be best to return to her life in New York.

But the change in location didn't solve her issues. Rosie's life progressively got worse. Instead of adjusting to the realities of what had happened with her children, Rosie began to be deeply affected by it. Before long, her relationship with Jim Miller ended. For the next two years, only her survival skills kept her afloat. She thought, *How could I get so far from reality? How could I get so sidetracked and miss out on the things that really matter?* She put all of her possessions in storage and walked away.

Over in Brooklyn, time was passing also. Mr. and Mrs. Haynes were still caring for Val and me. Just as Rosie had envisioned back in 1958, Val was attending Public School #3. In 1965, I started first grade there also.

For some time, Val had been trying to convince me that Mr. and Mrs. Haynes were not our parents. In my young mind, I just couldn't make the connection. I just could not see that they didn't look anything like me. One day, Val found a note that Momma Haynes had written back in the fall of 1958. But even with the evidence it contained, I wasn't convinced.

When I was in the second grade, my teacher said something that seemed very strange to me. "John," she said, "you need to let your parents know that you must use your correct last name."

That was a shock! My immediate response was, "What is my real last name?"

She had it written on a piece of paper that she bent down to show me. "Here it is, John. It's spelled L-o-m-a-c-a-n-g." I had to ask her how to pronounce it, so I could tell Momma and Papa when I got home. Even walking home that day with Val, it really didn't seem real. I did remember all the times my sister kept trying to convince me that the Hayneses were not our parents. Now I had to believe her. Now there was proof.

I ran into the house that day calling, "Papa! Momma! The teacher says that I have to use my real name."

George and Carmen looked at each other with an "I wonder what's next?" look. George asked, "John, what did your teacher say your real last name is?"

"She said it's spelled L-o-m-a-c-a-n-g."

Mr. Haynes sat me down and slowly said, "Yep. That's your real last name."

I was confused. "You mean that my name is *not* John Parker Haynes?"

"No. It's *John Parker Lomacang*!"

Val looked at me with a big smirk. Later she whispered, "See! I told you."

What an experience in the day of a seven-year-old! Go to school and, chances are, you'll learn more than you bargained for. That little bit of information started a fire in my heart that would only burn more intensely as the years went by. By 1967, I had been moved to a brand new school, Public School #56, just a few streets away from Madison Street. Val remained in Public School #3.

Sometimes when I came home from school, Val would tell me that my father had been there. I really didn't understand what she meant, because I never saw him. I remember Mr. Haynes telling me that someone had sent a new television there in my name, but he gave it back to the delivery person. I guess he figured that a "new television" was not proper compensation for all that he had done for my sister and me. I really can't fault him; I would have acted the same way.

Mrs. Haynes had a deep love for us. She was the true force behind her husband. Whatever we got that was substantial, she was the one behind it. Because of her love for us, even though she never worked outside the home, we were never in need of anything.

Papa worked at a stockbrokerage in the Wall Street area of downtown Manhattan. On many occasions, he brought home little gifts for us. He was a hard-working man and a patient man. He taught me how to paint, how to replace broken windows, how to fix broken locks, as well as how to install locks. His famous saying was "Every man should know how to use his hands." He also taught me the value of not being lazy. Every day we had specific chores to do, some even before we went to school. When we came home, he made sure that we completed our homework before anything else.

We knew that Papa loved us. It seemed to us that he was always striving to do his best. One thing was for certain: He was always pleased when we did well.

Sunday was the major cleaning day in our home. My sister vacuumed each of the rooms. I had to sweep each hallway floor, along with the steps from the fourth floor to the ground floor. One Sunday, I had my mind so focused on getting the job done in a hurry, that I tried to carry the bucket of water, the mop, the broom, and the dustpan down the stairs at the same time. As it happened, when I got to the top of the highest set of steps, I learned that rushing does not shorten a job. Let's put it this way: My balancing act lasted for two steps. I fell the rest of the way down the steps. Broom, mop, dustpan, and bucket (filled with water) came tumbling down the steps after me. The noise was nerve shattering. The aftermath was awful. There was water everywhere. Everyone thought that I had been hurt in the fall. But the only thing that hurt was being laughed at while I sat there on the floor, soaking wet with a broken ego.

Papa was also a man of discipline. To this day I cannot forget one occasion when my inquisitive nature got the best of me. One of Papa's great treasures was a gold pocket watch. Periodically, he would wear it. Sometimes he would just take it out of the drawer and look at it. The watch was quite old, or so it seemed to me. It had a porcelain face and a gold chain. I don't remember where he got the watch, but I do remember that on more than one occasion, he warned me not to play with it.

Let's just say that I had an "inquiring mind." I came home from school that day, and I could not get the watch out of my mind. I wanted to see what made it tick. Of course, that meant I had to open it. Now follow carefully. How does a mischievous little boy open a very expensive watch? I tried to open it with my fingers—that didn't work. So, I looked for a screwdriver. I thought that if I could get the screwdriver between the seams of the watch, I could pry it open. Guess what? That didn't work, either.

By now I was so engrossed in "accomplishing my mission" that I lost all sense of reason. I had to get this watch open. The subtle approach hadn't worked, so I resorted to the next level of strategy—get it open at any cost. Looking back, I wish I had understood what the word *cost* really meant. I found the only reasonable instrument that I thought would do the job. After all, if a hammer could not get a watch open, what could?

I knelt down on the bedroom floor and held the watch on its side with my left hand, while I raised the hammer with my right hand. While the hammer was on its way down, deep in the recesses of my mind I imagine that the Lord impressed me that this was not a good idea. Before I could reason it out, the loud crash of the hammer meeting the watch startled me back into reality. It was too late. I did accomplish my mission; the watch was open. I mean, the watch WAS OPEN! Pieces of the watch were flying in every direction. The porcelain face was in pieces. The glass was shattered. The hinge that held the cover of the watch together was broken. I saw the springs and all the intricate parts. Somehow, seeing them did not seem important anymore. My reason returned to me. How do I know, you ask? This is how; I knew that I was in trouble.

Momma Haynes was in the kitchen. She called out, "John, what was that noise?"

"Nothing, Momma," I quickly replied. Then I started gathering the pieces together. I could not risk having Papa finding his watch like this. I reasoned to myself, *It's better that he not find it at all than find it in this condition.*

Why is it that when we get scared or nervous, we do foolish things? Why is it that children think they could "pull one over" on adults? Where did the idea come from that adults are not wise enough to put "two and two together"?

I don't know the answer to all of the above questions, but I do know that when I saw the watch *after* I hit it, knowing the answers was not important. I devised a foolproof plan, or so I thought. I hid the watch and all of its pieces under the dresser that was next to Papa's bed. Then I ran out of the house as fast as my feet could carry me. I wanted to make sure that when Papa came home, he would not see me in the vicinity of his dresser.

A few hours passed, and I became so engrossed in playing baseball in the street out in front of the house that I all but forgot the earlier incident. True to his daily routine, Papa came around the corner from Classon Avenue and turned onto Madison Street. When he saw me, he greeted me as usual. Papa liked to call me Junior. "Junior, did you do your homework yet?"

"Sure did!" I called.

"When you are done, come in the house and show it to me."

"OK, Papa. I'll be there soon."

I went right along as if I was out of the woods. It wasn't long before I heard Papa's voice. "Junior . . . come here now!" I ran into the house so as not to act suspicious. When I came inside, I saw Papa standing with his back to me. He was looking down at his hand as if he was engrossed in something. When he turned around, I should have confessed. I should have thrown myself on the "mercy of the court." But I waited for the next question to see if I was in the clear. Papa asked, "Did you see my gold watch?"

This was the pivotal point. This was the answer that would decide my fate. This was the moment of truth. The scales of justice were being weighed, and I was on the wrong side. At that moment, I think I saw my life flash in front of my eyes.

It seemed as though the world slowed down as I answered him. "No, Papa, I–did–not–see–your–watch."

WRONG ANSWER! Papa slowly revealed his hand that had been hidden behind his back. Before he opened it, I knew what I was going to see. Somehow, the watch looked much worse than I remembered. Papa asked another question, "Do you know anything about this?" I had been given a second chance, and I was too dumb to see it. Again my answer was wrong. "No, Papa, I don't know anything about that. I was outside."

By then Momma had heard the conversation, and she came into the room. She was the last person that I needed to see. Looking at me standing in front of her husband, she said, "Junior, do you remember when I asked you what that loud noise was, and you told me Nothing? Do you remember that?"

I replied, "Yes, I remember." At that moment, I wished that I had not touched the watch. Frankly, I went so far as to wish I had never seen it, period! But all the wishing in the world was not going to change the facts. I WAS BUSTED!

Papa resumed his questioning as he removed his belt from his pants. At that point, I knew that the verdict was in. In the final analysis, there was only one logical conclusion, anyway. First of all, my sister would not have broken the watch. Second, there was no one else in the house who could be considered the culprit. Finally, I was known to be mischievous. Suffice it to say, that day lives on "in infamy" in my brain.

Some of the most fun Papa and I had together was when it snowed. New York is notorious for large snowfalls. Papa had more than one pair of heavy boots, the kind designed so you could put your foot and shoe in at the same time. Normally, he wasn't much for taking pictures, but when the snowfalls came through, for some reason he didn't mind posing with his shovel and his big boots. We have a picture of Papa, Val, and me standing in front of the house, posing in the cold.

I particularly liked snow, because frequently school would be canceled. Whenever it snowed, we would wake up early to sit by the radio, waiting for the news about school closings. I also liked the snow because I could go to the neighbors and shovel their snow for a small price.

The times I spent with Papa were times for building strong relationships. I didn't just learn how to "do things." I learned life-shaping principles that would remain with me. Papa was at least two things to me. He was the man I needed to learn to be and the father that God gave me. He showed me the strong side of love, while his wife showed me the softer side of love. I now look back and understand more clearly why a home with a father and mother is God's plan.

Mr. and Mrs. Hayneses' adopted son, Kelvin, was older than we were. As far as we were concerned, he was our only brother. It is amazing to Val and me how the Lord gave us a family when we didn't have one. We learned that family is not always those who are naturally connected. Family to us was a patchwork quilt. We had uncles, aunts, cousins, and nieces that were not related to us through our bloodline; they were related to us through Momma and Papa.

Kelvin didn't live with us, but he visited frequently. One memorable occasion was Christmas Eve. This was in the days when we actually believed in Santa Claus. We didn't know that each Christmas Eve Papa and Momma put our gifts under the tree after we went to bed.

On this occasion, Kelvin was appointed as the watch dog to make sure we went to sleep. We knew something was fishy, because he kept checking on us. I decided to investigate. I sneaked up the steps as silently as I could. When I was at the top of the stairs, I saw them bringing box after box in through the front door of the house. I also saw a brand new three-speed bicycle. As I was checking it out, my foot slipped and knocked against the steps. Kelvin turned to look. He didn't see anything, but he headed my way. I ran down the steps in my bare feet as quietly as I could.

Fortunately, I got back to bed before Kelvin got to my room. But he tricked me. He called out quietly, "John, are you sleeping?"

I didn't think. I just yelled back, "Yes!"

As soon as the word was out of my mouth, I realized that I was busted. Kelvin laughed out loud, having solved the mystery of the sound on the steps.

The next morning, Papa sat us down and told us that there is no such thing as Santa Claus. We felt good, because up to that point, we actually did not know whom we were to thank for all of those gifts. From that day on, we gained a deeper appreciation for Momma and Papa. We saw that their love for us was greater than we had realized.

Kelvin was the apple of their eye. Whatever he wanted, they tried their best to furnish for him. Momma tried for years to get him to give his life to the Lord. He had been raised in the church but left after he was in his early twenties. I realize that she took a different approach with my sister and me. Instead of trying to get us to go to church, she taught us at home about the Lord. Through her life—the way she lived and the way she loved—she showed us the blessings of the Lord. She found joy in teaching us the principles of life.

Some evenings, Momma let us lean against her shoulders as we sat on the couch and she read the Bible to us. When she sat at the piano, she invited us to sit with her on the bench. Her favorite song was "Sweet Hour of Prayer." Although I learned how to play other songs on the piano, "Sweet Hour of Prayer" still reminds me of sitting in the living room with Momma sitting to my left while she played and sang that song.

I have come to realize that my view of God was being shaped by the characteristics I saw in the Hayneses—especially Papa. I learned that coming to God, as my divine Father, is nothing that I need to be afraid of. When Papa accepted me with my faults, I later understood that my heavenly Father does also. When Papa did not allow my mistakes to separate me from him, I was able to more easily come to my heavenly Father and know that coming to Him is not conditional. My acceptance is not based on my perfection but on His love. Just as with Papa, God accepts me as I am, but He never leaves me the way He finds me. Thank the Lord that He sent Mr. Haynes when I needed a father to see me through. My heavenly Father provided an earthly father to help me understand the love of my heavenly Father.

CHAPTER THREE

My Anchors

From the earliest days I can remember, church was part of the intricate fabric of my life. We lived less than a mile from the Bethel Seventh-day Adventist Church, in Brooklyn, New York. This beautiful sanctuary featured stained-glass windows, tall ceilings with hanging chandeliers, five red-carpeted aisles, and a pipe organ that dominated the front wall. Most of the time, we walked to church. And if we arrived much past 10:00 a.m., it was difficult to find seats together; the church was so full.

The church service there was awe-inspiring. Its African-American, predominately West Indian, congregation brought a rich sense of church traditions. I remember so well the song that was played as the minister prepared to enter: "The Lord Is in His Holy Temple." The atmosphere was so still you could hear your heart beat. As the minister entered, before him and behind him was a retinue of elders, deacons, and deaconesses.

In our culture, the men wore dark suits, and the women wore white outfits with white hats. They looked so uniformed and so "holy" that as a young child, I thought I might see God at any moment. Behind the minister's seat, the choir loft was filled with a hundred singers in blue satin robes with a gold cloth neckband. When the organist played the congregational hymn, the whole building resonated with voices singing and instruments playing to the glory of God. It was often half-past noon before the minister began his sermon, which sometimes lasted over an hour. Still, when church was over, people lingered for a long while to talk with each other.

Although Papa didn't attend church, we were there with Momma Haynes every week. And when we went to church, we stayed all day. Most of the other families did also. We joined together in the fellowship room upstairs to eat the lunches we had brought. After lunch, we stayed by to talk, sing, read the Bible, and just have a "good time." Our church was very family oriented.

I practically grew up in the Bethel church. I think I know every nook and cranny in that building. I loved to go to the basement, which was directly under the sanctuary. From there, you could really hear the organ. Of course, the basement and pipes that crisscrossed it were covered with dust.

One day during the service, I went on my usual "safari" to the basement. What I didn't know was that the church deacons were watching. I was in the very back of the basement when I heard footsteps behind me. I quickly hid in one of the supply cabinets. When I heard no other sounds, I opened the cabinet door to find the basement dark—pitch dark. The deacons had turned out the lights.

Even though I was in the church, I was terrified of the dark. Forgetting my white shirt, suit, and tie, I had only one thought, *I need to get out of here quickly!* For some reason, I remember that day clearly. In my rush to get out, I ran into everything imaginable, falling time after time. I know I fell onto a heap of sand, because falling face first was the only thing that stopped my shouting for help.

I thought I would never get out. The organ playing above me confused me, and I heard footsteps all around me in the dark. When I finally found the basement door, it was locked! My next move was not well-thought out. I began to bang on the door and yell with all my energy. Finally, I heard keys jingling and knew I was being rescued. But when the door opened, it wasn't just the deacon. Momma Haynes was there.

The deacon's smirk said, "I finally got you." Momma did not have a smirk on her face. She had a "your life is at an end" look. She grabbed me by my ears (not hard to do, if you know me) and led me through the hall, up two flights of stairs, and into the midst of the church service. I thought she would let my ear go when we entered the sanctuary, but she did not. Our seat was on the second row from the front. Momma was on a mission to make sure that I learned a valuable lesson, and she succeeded. It was one of my most embarrassing moments in church. I looked as if I had just ridden to church on the back of a wild horse. It took a few months for me to live that one down.

Bethel church was the place where I learned some of the most valuable lessons in life. Once when Val and I were sent to church alone, we were given offering money. I played with my quarter and nickel all the way to church. When we sat down, Val hissed at me to stop, because the coins were too noisy. So I did something quieter—I put the coins in my mouth. I kept shuffling them over and under my tongue. I overlooked the taste of the metal (and the hygiene), because I was absorbed in my game. But the inevitable happened—I swallowed the nickel. I felt it going down and sat up quickly. As soon as I did, my sister turned and pinched me. "You swallowed it, didn't you? I told you not to play with it in church."

I felt the nickel making its way down. In about a minute my stomach began to hurt. When the offering bucket came by, I faithfully put in my twenty-five cents. Oh, how I would have loved to put in thirty cents. I never saw that nickel again. But I've always thought that I'm worth at least five cents more than the average person!

I gave my heart to Christ and was baptized in that church when I was nine years old. My love for church began there, and so did my love for music. Momma had bought me a little guitar that I learned to play. At one of my first musical performances, Val and I and two other children were supposed to sing for the evening service. Apparently, I started playing, but when the others began to sing, I stopped and just stood there and cried—a young victim of stage fright.

I remember glorious church picnics—sometimes it took twenty buses to carry everyone to the park. And camp meeting at Victory Lake is a special memory, especially the year we stayed all ten days in a yellow canvas tent. As I grew older, church began to mean more. It was no longer "go because you have to." I went because I wanted to. Momma had laid a strong foundation, and no matter how old I got, what I had learned in church stayed with me. As the years went by, church was the hedge that kept me from going to extremes in my choices.

Although our church had a school, my sister and I went to public school. This created a constant "tug-of-war" in our actions and emotions. After fifth grade, I attended Macon Junior High School. It was the worst school experience I ever had. Small "cliques" and gangs began to form almost immediately. Everyone joined one, if only for the security. There were daily fights, sometimes between students and teachers. Fires were set in trash cans and lockers.

I was teased and picked on more than I care to mention—all because I refused to join one of the gangs. Eating in the cafeteria was a risk, because food was constantly thrown around the room. I was hit by milk containers, partially eaten apples, cake, etc. We were given bus passes to ride the city buses to school, but before the first two weeks were up, my bus pass was taken by another student. I was so afraid to go to school that I complained to Mr. Haynes. He came to the school to try to resolve my difficulties, but nothing changed. So, I took matters into my own hands—I just decided to skip school.

I would leave home as expected and just not go to school. Some days I would ride the subway all day. Since I arrived home at the expected time, no one suspected anything. By that time, Momma had become ill, and she couldn't keep up with our growing demands. My sister was in New Utrecht High School, three grades ahead of me. Some days I would end up at her school. She assumed it was just a rare thing, so she never reported this to Momma and Papa.

Often I went to one of the famous amusement parks in Brooklyn—Coney Island. Sometimes the carnies would let me work for a few hours to earn a little money to enjoy. Other times I would go to Prospect Park, one of the big parks off Eastern Parkway, in Brooklyn. One day, Papa got on the subway car that I was riding. Fortunately, I was at the other end of the car. I got off at the next stop.

One day when I arrived home, Papa had an unusual look on his face—the kind of look that told me something was wrong. "So you went to school today, huh?" he asked, staring at me with one eye closed. I tried to figure out what was going on. It didn't take long. Papa pulled a small folded envelope out of his shirt pocket and unfolded the letter close to my face. "Explain this!"

Of course, it was a letter from the school about my absences. I assured him that it was some kind of mistake. He looked at me. "Are you sure? Tomorrow I will go with you to school to straighten this out."

I knew I was in deep trouble. The next morning, breakfast tasted like the last meal before execution. Before long, we were sitting in the principal's office. He reported that I had been absent from school for forty-two days. FORTY-TWO DAYS!

That evening at home was not the most pleasant. Let's just say that Papa made it difficult for me to sit down. I explained that I was afraid to go to school. "You should have come to me for help," he said. Hearing where I had been instead of school didn't make things any easier. Needless to say, I missed no more days that year.

One other issue had to be resolved. When my sister found out that my bus pass had been stolen, she came to school with me the next morning. Before the bell sounded, kids hung out playing basketball, listening to music, smoking, or whatever. "Who took your bus pass?" Val asked. I pointed to Gerald, who was leaning up against the school wall with a smirk on his face. Remember that Brooklyn in those days was a tough place. If you didn't stand up for yourself, you were pegged as a pushover, and more people would take advantage of you. My sister loved me, but she was tough. Val wasn't going to let her little brother be seen as a pushover. In her way of urging me to stand up for myself, she said, "If you don't go over there and hit him, I'm going to hit you!"

Well, I was not about to be beat-up by my sister. I walked over to Gerald by myself. As far as he knew, I was alone, so he took up where he left off, trying to force his hands in my pocket to see if I had any money or if I had another bus pass. But when he reached for my pocket, I balled-up my fist and punched him in the chest as hard as I could. Before he could hit me back, my big sister was right there to defend me.

I made up my mind not to be a pushover anymore. And over the years, my sister and I have always defended each other.

Considering all this, it was no surprise that when the school year ended, I was left back. The teacher had already informed me that I would be staying in grade six for another six months. But I rushed home on the day report cards were due and intercepted it. I carefully erased the assigned grade for the next year and wrote in "Seventh." I didn't realize the school had already phoned Momma to discuss it. When she confronted my deception, for once I admitted the truth.

"Do you want to go back to that school next year?" she asked.

My answer came quickly. "No, I don't."

"Tomorrow I will talk to George about putting you in Bethel Seventh-day Adventist School."

Suddenly, my summer looked much brighter. I was also able to get a job at a grocery store stocking shelves and doing other little odds and ends. I didn't earn much, but at the end of each day, at closing time, the storeowner told me that I could take a bag of groceries home. I learned a lot that summer, and by the end, I had earned enough trust to run the cash register.

One of the most important values I learned from Momma and Papa was the value of work—instead of waiting for handouts, you work for what you want. They also taught me how to handle the money I earned, including the practice of putting money aside for the Lord. Momma never allowed us to go to church with empty hands. She said that the

Lord was to be first. Even when Momma bought us new dressy clothes, she would say, "Wear it to church first before you wear it anywhere else."

My first day at church school was an eye opener. Unlike public school, everyone at Bethel wore uniforms—white shirts and black pants, with maroon jackets and ties. The school was small in comparison to junior high, and with daily prayer and worship, the atmosphere was very different. The only time we prayed in public school was in an emergency! Bethel helped me understand prayer as a way of life. I have forgotten the few friends I made in public school, but many of the friends I made at Bethel during my seventh- and eighth-grade years are still my friends today.

My first year at Bethel was a bittersweet year. The sweet side was that I got to attend church school. The bitter side was that Mrs. Haynes died that same year, 1971. Momma had battled with a diseased kidney for some time, and it just got progressively worse. During the year, she became progressively immobile. Val now cooked, and I had to do more cleaning to take up the slack. We went to church without her, but we always brought home the church bulletin, so she could keep up with things that happened in church. It was hard to go without her. Some days, we stopped just long enough to be seen and collect the bulletin before we left.

Some Sabbaths after church communion, the elders and deaconesses of the church would come to our home and administer the ordinances to Momma. It was obvious that Momma would not last much longer. Val and I were about to lose the only mother we really had ever known.

As her health failed, I would often sit across the room on my bed and look at her, remembering the times we had shared. I remember her comforting hugs during thunderstorms, my licking the cake pan when she was baking, the picnics in Prospect Park, singing with her in church, attending Victory Lake camp meetings together, Thanksgiving dinners, decorating the Christmas tree, and opening the gifts. She would pray with me and tell me that the Lord had a plan for my life. She told me that if I would be faithful, one day I would make her proud.

What would we do without Momma? How would Papa manage to raise us without her? To whom would Val turn for the motherly advice she would need? I was just twelve years old, and Val was fifteen. Papa was going on sixty-one. He needed his wife, and we needed our mother.

Momma was finally admitted into Cumberland Hospital, in downtown Brooklyn. At that time, there was an age restriction for visitors, and I was too young to go upstairs to see her. After a few times of sitting alone in the waiting room, I asked to stay home when Papa and Val visited her. Early one evening, the phone rang. Things were not looking good. Papa and Val immediately took a cab to the hospital. I was told to stay home. I stayed in the backyard shooting hoops with my undersized ball and the small rim over the back door. Hours passed, and I didn't hear anything.

I didn't hear Papa and Val return. I just remember the back door being pushed open. I stopped shooting to see Val wiping her eyes. I almost instantly began to cry too. All I remember is her saying, "Momma passed away. She told me to tell you that she prayed for you." We hugged and cried together. Papa just sat at the dinner table with tears in his eyes. That evening the house was quiet. But some distant family members who lived on the third floor began making phone calls the next day. It was announced in church, and then it seemed as if the doorbell was ringing all day and evening.

Momma had been a faithful deaconess in her church. We thought that the church would be packed for her funeral. Unfortunately, camp meeting had just begun, and many members and the pastor were away. We hoped the pastor would return to perform the funeral, but he could not get away from his duties. The service was performed by one of the church elders. This upset my sister and Papa very much. They felt that the pastor should have been there, because Momma was so faithful to the church. Because of this, my sister's heart was soured against church, and before long, she stopped attending.

I had one more year of school at Bethel. Val was in Greater New York Academy, in Queens, New York. After tenth grade, she went back to public school. That proved to be a major turning point in her life. After Momma died, our entire outlook on life changed drastically. Momma had been our spiritual anchor. Papa had all but shut down. He was gone a lot, and when we asked him how he felt, he would only say that he missed his wife. We missed her, too, but life had to go on. We knew that if Momma were still alive, she would want us to do our best. Val and I were determined to do just that, but the world seemed to have other plans.

CHAPTER FOUR

"How Did You Know?"

One evening later that year, the house was filled with music and laughter. As they often did, Papa and his cousins were in the kitchen playing guitars, drinking whiskey, laughing, and talking the night away. Their good old West Indian Calypso music stirred up my interest in the guitar.

On this early fall evening, I wanted to get out of the house and do something else. With Papa's OK, I put on my coat and headed to my friend's house next door. It was a little past sunset, so the streetlight in front of our house was on. As I opened the front-yard gate, I noticed that a big, shiny black, four-door Fleetwood Cadillac was parked on the street. I paid no attention to the person in it, because he did not look familiar to me. What I didn't know was that the person who was in it was paying particular attention to me.

All of a sudden I heard a voice. "Hello there!" a man called. I stopped and turned to see if he was talking to me. "Your name must be John," the man continued.

"Yes, it is."

"I'm Johnny," he said. Then he went on. "Your sister's name is Vivian, and you are about thirteen, and she is about sixteen years old."

"Yes," I replied. By then he had my undivided attention. He was making me very nervous.

"Your birthday is . . . and hers is . . ." He named the correct dates as I stood there stunned. He still had one foot on the pavement and the other in the car.

I had to ask the question, "How do you know?"

He put both feet on the pavement, placed his hands on his knees, and leaned forward. In a confident voice he said, "I'm your father!"

Even in the dim light, I could see that he was somewhat uncomfortable. I quickly replied, "No, you're not. My father is in the house." Before he could reply, I turned and ran back inside the house. I ran right into the kitchen yelling, "Papa, Papa, there's a man outside who says he is my father!"

It was as if the power button on a stereo had turned off—the laughing, talking, and guitar playing came to an abrupt halt as everyone turned and stared. Only Papa spoke. "What are you talking about?"

I said it again. "There's a man outside who told me that he is my father!"

Papa had a disgusted look as he asked, "Did he tell you his name?"

"He said that his name is Johnny!" I answered.

Everyone watched Papa's response. He braced himself to stand up and quietly said, "Yep, that's your father." In the commotion that created, the doorbell rang. Val ran to the front door. There stood the man called Johnny. Papa called out, "Just a minute. I'm opening the door."

Johnny was well-dressed in his dark wool coat, dark suit, white shirt, and tie. He had wavy black hair and was well-groomed and clean-shaven. I could smell his cologne as he took off his coat. He put out his hand and said, "Hi, Mister Haynes."

Papa shook his hand slowly. "It's been a long time since I've seen you. What brings you around?"

"I heard that Mrs. Haynes passed away a few months ago," Johnny answered, "and I wanted to see how things were."

Val and I just sat and stared. I was so stunned that I forgot to take my coat off. Val nudged me as if to say, "See, I told you that Papa was

"HOW DID YOU KNOW?"

not your father." I had so many questions that I did not know where to begin, so I just let my two "fathers" talk. All I could think was "Wow! I have two fathers!"

Johnny suggested that we go out to "Juniors," a well-known restaurant in downtown Brooklyn, famous for its cheesecake. Papa informed his company that he would be back, and the four of us went out. Johnny unlocked his car and opened the doors for us. He and Papa sat in the front seat. I sat in the seat behind Papa, so I could look at my "new father."

At the restaurant we were all nervous, even Johnny. Finally, he turned to me and asked, "So how have you been?" Before I could respond, another question followed, "What grade are you in?"

"Seventh," I awkwardly replied. He turned to Val and asked her the same question. Just then they brought our cheesecake (I had a strawberry milkshake also).

We sat and talked for over an hour before Papa said, "I have to get back to the house. I have company." Johnny reached into his pocket to pay the bill. As he did, he gave Val and me $20 bills. Looking back, I guess that was his way of trying to gain instant favor with us or maybe to soften the impact of just showing up after thirteen years. Whatever the reason might have been, I took the money, and so did my sister. Papa just looked on.

On the way out, Johnny asked if I would like to sit up front. As we pulled away, he smiled and asked, "Did you know that your first and middle name is my first and last name?"

"I guess so" was all I could think to say.

Back at home, Johnny came in and talked with me for a little while longer. "If you're not busy after school tomorrow, I would like to take you to Queens to see your grandmother. Then, if we have time, maybe we could go shopping for a while."

I wasn't going to object to anything that he suggested. I'd wished for my real father most of my life, and now that he was back, I was certainly not going to do anything to make him want to leave. "What time could you come to pick me up?"

"Is four o'clock OK with Mr. Haynes?"

I ran to ask Papa, and he consented. "I'll see you tomorrow then, Dad—I mean Johnny."

He knew that the situation was uncomfortable. "If you want to call me Johnny, that's OK with me." He turned to Papa and said, "Thanks." Papa just nodded his head without saying a word. I followed him to the door, and after he left, Papa just went back to the kitchen without saying a word.

The next day, Johnny took Val and me to Queens to meet his mother. She lived near Shea Stadium, where the New York Mets baseball team plays. When we arrived, Johnny said, "John, meet your grandmother, Mrs. Nurse."

She had a strong stare, as if she were trying to look through me. Then she slowly and softly said to Johnny, "So, this is your son." She seemed nice but vague. That evening I asked her if she knew about my mother. "I met her only once," she replied. "Your father kept her a secret."

After we left, I asked my dad more directly about what had happened with my mother. He told me that they were never married. He said that he and Rosie (he called her Kim) met in a club where he was a musician. They met, dated, and then moved in together. He told me that they did not stay together long. When I asked him why, he just said, "It didn't work out."

I kept asking questions, because information about so much of my life was missing. But the more I asked about my mother, the more evasive he became. I finally saw that it was an uncomfortable subject for him, so I stopped prodding. I did ask one important question before I stopped. "When was the last time you saw her?"

Johnny answered, "I saw her on television in the 1960s modeling stockings." His answer left a big hole in my expectations. I figured that since I had met my father, I would have all the answers I needed. Instead, I had more questions than ever.

For some time my dad, Johnny, was involved in my life. He took me to his apartment—I never forgot the address: 104 Martense Street,

"HOW DID YOU KNOW?"

in the Flatbush section of Brooklyn, New York. His apartment walls were lined with black-and-white photos. I was fascinated to learn that he had taken all of the photos. He had pictures of some very famous people on his wall. I can only recall a few names, such as the world-champion boxer, Mohammed Ali, the renowned jazz great Duke Ellington, and other jazz artists like Dizzy Gillespie and Brooks Kerr. He also had a picture of a well-known female jazz singer named Dakota Staton. What was even more amazing to me was when he told me that he knew her personally. When I asked what he meant, he replied, "We've been seeing each other a short while."

My dad had lived a single man's life for so long that I did not see how he could possibly fit me in. I entertained the idea of living with him. When I asked him about that possibility, he said, "My life is so busy I would not have time to raise you. You are better off staying with Mr. Haynes." Although that was not what I wanted to hear, I had to agree with him.

I wanted Johnny to give some direction to my life, but it just did not seem to be a priority to him. He was so accustomed to living for himself that he would not even consent for me to spend one night at his apartment. There was always an excuse.

On the other hand, I did learn a few valuable lessons from him. I remember my dad talking to me about choices. He asked, "Who are your friends?" When I told him who they were and what they spent their time doing, he said, "If you want to get somewhere in life, you have to hang out with people who are where you want to be." He told me that I would never be anything other than what my friends were.

At the time it didn't register, but a short while later, I took his advice. I started exploring Manhattan much more than before. I began to see that the world was much larger than my little corner in Brooklyn. Johnny contributed to the "expansion of my understanding of the city" by frequently inviting me to visit him at the place where he worked. He was the main musical act at a club called Chelsea's Place in downtown Manhattan. I often went to the club because that was the easiest way to find him.

My dad was very outgoing. There was not a shy bone in his body. He taught me how to be more confident. He said, "When you meet people, look them in the eye when you speak to them." He was a role model to me in several areas. But more than anything else, I wanted his dedication and undivided attention. I found out to my sorrow that those were things I could not have.

I was caught between my past and my future, and the more time that went by, the more difficult it became to mesh the two. I did not want to disrespect Papa, the man who raised me, by getting too excited about Johnny, my natural father. There were days when I knew that Papa was disgusted. He wouldn't say much, but when he did, it was a comment like, "If you need money, let your father give you some."

I tried not to let it bother me. To some degree, I was able to understand how he felt when he heard Johnny accepting complements like "How nice your son is!" How would you feel if you raised a boy for thirteen years only to have someone else get the credit for what a good son he turned out to be?

I imagine that Papa spent some time looking back over the thirteen years of sacrifice, hard-earned money, sweat, tears, painstaking labor, and relationship building only to feel greatly unappreciated. On the other hand, I imagine that he also thought of the void that we were filling in his life. After all, he did not have any children of his own. He could have seen all his efforts as a small investment in filling his life with meaning and giving him and his wife someone to live for and love.

My father made some attempts to patch things up with me. The reality is that no matter what he did, there was really no way to balance the picture after thirteen years. However, he did try. Johnny took me to one of his favorite men's clothing stores and bought me a wool coat. Then we spent the day together in Manhattan. I was so anxious to know my father that whatever he wanted to do was fine with me, as long as I could be with him. I had already figured out that I would not get everything I desired, so I settled for what I was able to get.

Even though Johnny was not around much of my life, I applaud him for having the courage to come back, even if it was thirteen years later. He didn't have to come back at all. I didn't know him, and some

"HOW DID YOU KNOW?"

men would have been happy to leave well enough alone. When I asked him why he came back, his answer just did not make sense to me. He told me that he came back because he heard that Mrs. Haynes had died. It seemed to me that if he cared about our wellbeing, he would have returned many years earlier. In the end, however, it's not important that it make sense to me as long as it was sufficient for him.[1]

1972—the year that I graduated from the eighth grade at Bethel Seventh-day Adventist School. The year since Mrs. Haynes had died was a growing time in my life. It was the last year of church school, but I made a true friend that year—Cedric Walker. Ricky invited me to his home for lunch after church on occasion, and his family always made me feel welcome.

The summer Mrs. Haynes died, Ricky and his family were in a terrible accident on the way to camp meeting. Not long after that, his mother contracted cancer. A year later, she died. Since we were so close before the accident, we were even closer after the death of his mother. It began a friendship that has lasted the rest of my life. Shortly after Ricky's mother passed away, he decided to move in with me. Fifteen Madison Street was a four-story house that had individual rooms for rent on the two upper floors. Ricky moved in to room 3. After we graduated from Bethel school, he went to Brooklyn Tech High School, and I went to James Madison; both were in Brooklyn.

We were more than friends; we were like brothers. We attended the same church, lived in the same house, had the same friends, and shared in the good and bad times of life. Both of us were quite independent. After Papa lost his wife, he left it up to Val and me to provide for the things we wanted. Papa would provide for our "necessities," as he put it. Anything else that we needed was up to us. Work was a given. Val, Ricky, and I had to make up our minds whether to sink or swim. The days of relying on parents were in the past. We had to push ourselves to achieve educationally and financially. I have learned that there is no greater drive than when you are pushed to survive.

In our second year of high school, my life began to take a new path. Since Mrs. Haynes died, Val and I lost the spiritual focus of our lives. Momma was the one that made sure we stayed connected to the church. She was the anchor that kept us from drifting off into the paths of indiscretion. My sister left the church shortly after 1971. She dove into the party and nightlife of New York City. Since she was older than I, I followed her lead.

I remember well the party days. My sister met friends in her high school who greatly influenced her direction. Wherever there was a party, we went. It did not matter how cold it was or how many trains we had to take; we were there. My sister began frequenting clubs where live music was played. It was around the time that the "Saturday Night Fever" pitch was at its height. Most of the places she went for partying were for "over 21" crowds. Val had friends that got her in, and she got me in. The party life began to consume us, but at that time, we didn't see anything wrong with it. We were just having a "good time."

I was so captivated by the excitement that I wanted to get even more involved. I wanted to become a DJ—a disc jockey. I spent the money I was earning buying sound equipment—records, speakers, turntables, microphones, and whatever else I fancied. The strange thing is that I did not completely leave the church. I still attended, though less and less frequently. Every now and then I would go, just to see how my friends were. It became more of a casual hangout than a place of worship for me. And if that were not bad enough, many of my church friends were also in the same party circles that I frequented. We kind of "kept each other's secrets." When I worked the church service as an usher, I would slip party fliers in the church bulletins that I handed to my friends. I now look back on that and thank God that He was patient with me. I have come to understand that God sees us for what we can become and not only for what we are.

At sixteen years old, I was on Broadway and Forty-sixth Street spinning records at the Seafood Playhouse—a club for those twenty-five years old and over. My party schedule was from Thursdays to Sundays usually. I was also learning how to play billiards. My time was consumed with partying and playing pool. My standard daily equipment was a billiard cue and a "boom box."

I learned many vices in public school. Thankfully, I did not smoke. I drank alcohol on a casual basis, mostly when I was at a club or disco. In the midst of all of this carousing, I was still going to school, and I was getting good grades. Amazing!

I tried to get into sports in high school. I tried out for the varsity basketball team, the football team, and baseball team. I discovered quickly that at 6'2", 155 pounds, I was not built for football. The basketball games were held mostly on Friday nights and Saturdays, and for some reason, I couldn't play basketball then. I even tried out for baseball on a Saturday morning, but my conscience bothered me so much that I couldn't catch or run. When I got home, I vowed never again to go to a sporting event on the Sabbath. The strangest thing is, I was still partying. I know; it doesn't make sense to me, either.

Since I was accountable to no one and responsible for no one else, there seemed to be no immediate consequences for my choices. I just didn't think about what could happen—I just did my thing.

On the other hand, the Lord was still coming after me. He did not forget me, even though I had turned my back on the things I knew were right. I had my share of questions about the things I was taught to believe. The summer before tenth grade, I went looking for answers. I was looking for a church where I could attend and still be comfortable with my secular lifestyle.

I went to a Nazarene church that was one block from where I lived. Since the Sabbath was a major issue for me, I decided to ask the youth pastor to help me sort it out. After a youth group meeting, I asked him to explain what he believed about the Sabbath. Keep in mind I was the youth; he was the pastor. I asked, "Could you please explain to me what the Bible teaches about the Sabbath?"

His face went from pleasant to agitated. He said, "Don't you ever come back here!" I was honestly seeking, but he was not having any of it. I didn't immediately understand his anger over the Sabbath question, so I just chalked it up as a bad experience.

The Lord knew that I was searching. I had been raised to believe certain things, but as I got older, that was not good enough. I had to know *why* I believed *what* I believed. I knew that Momma Haynes was sincere, but I had to understand for myself where these beliefs came from. I wanted to know whether or not they were true. Even as I write these words, I am still amazed how the Lord worked on me.

I asked the same question of a Pentecostal pastor and a Catholic priest. The Pentecostal pastor said, "Don't tell me that the Sabbath was changed in 321 A.D. by Roman Emperor Constantine."

Shocked, I replied, "You know? Why aren't you telling your members the truth?" He gave me an angry look and stormed out, rudely leaving me sitting in his office.

The only one who told me the truth about the change of the Sabbath was a neighborhood priest I had known for years. We had such a good relationship that I felt I could ask him, "Father John, why do so many go to church on Sunday?"

He said, "Because our church changed it to that day."

Then I asked, "Why don't they change it back?"

"It's too far gone to change it now," he answered with a smile.

Back then I didn't think of asking him why he did not change. But I appreciated his honesty. Since then, I've been amazed to see how clearly information about the Sabbath comes from history books and the Bible. If you look up just five terms in any dictionary—*Saturday, Sunday, Sabbath, First day,* and *Seventh day*—you will get all of the historical answers on the subject you need. I am amazed at how many people read the Bible and see that the seventh day is the Sabbath but then fail to look at the calendar to see which day is the seventh. One person told me, "If I had just looked at the calendar years ago, I would have known the truth about the day the Lord blessed."

---

[1] A short bio of his musical accomplishments appears in the Appendix.

CHAPTER FIVE

God and His Lovely Assistant

In 1973, when I was fifteen, I began to notice a beautiful girl who came to our church. Sometimes when she and her sister arrived late and stood at the back of the church waiting to be seated, I would stare at them and marvel at how pretty they were. They were "intimidatingly" beautiful.

In other words, I was afraid to approach them. A few times I imagined how nice it would be to meet them, but I immediately put the idea out of my mind, because I felt they would not think much of me. After all, in our church of 1,200, there were many guys my age to catch her eye.

One Saturday evening, I came to the church during the evening program—it was primarily for young people. Bethel was the kind of church where people dressed very well to attend. It was not mandatory; I think it was more cultural. I came to the meeting in jeans and a green army jacket I had embroidered with blue yarn. I didn't know she was going to be there. And I didn't know my good friend, Chris Beaumont, was also a friend of hers.

After the meeting, the young people always stayed by and talked. But what happened that evening threw me into a tailspin. Chris approached me and said, "I have someone who wants to meet you." Naturally, I asked who it was. He said, "My friend Angie and her cousin Shirley." I asked him to point them out. When he pointed, I got instantly nervous. The very girl I had my eyes on was the one who wanted "to meet me!" I was shocked, and Chris knew it. He said to me, "They just want to meet you. They're not asking to date you." I calmed down a little bit and went with him.

"John, this is Angie and Shirley; this is John." Chris left the next move up to me. He knew that I was nervous, and so did they.

I could not let them get the upper hand, so I acted as "cool" as I could. "Hi," was all I could think to say. My throat was dry, my hands were fidgety, and my ears were getting red. Angie and Shirley just sat there looking pretty and smiling at me. Angie had light hazel-colored eyes and a pretty face. She just sat there, and I just looked with awe. I don't remember much of what we talked about, but I do remember that our conversation ended abruptly with the announcement, "Shirley, your father is here to pick you up!"

Angie asked me to walk her to the car. I was excited, but I played it off like it was no big thing. As I walked them over to the blue Dodge two-door, Angie threw me a kiss and told me to call her. I yelled, "I don't have your number!" She scribbled it on a small piece of paper and threw it out the car window. As the car drove off, I stood there stunned.

When I got home that night, I called her. Angie was surprised to hear from me so soon. She invited me to her home to meet her family. Needless to say, I could not wait.

A few days later, I went to her house. It was a shock—she didn't tell me she had five brothers! After I met her sister, Lecia, and her brothers Glen, Cliff, Heaton, and Ken, I found out that Angie had two sisters—she was the youngest of eight. We were now both sixteen years old and in the tenth grade. She went to Bay Ridge, an all girls' high school.

It was a wonderful evening. The house was full of people, but the family made me feel very comfortable. We watched television and talked all evening. Her brother Cliff wrestled with me as if he had known me for years. Angie's mother was so kind and gracious.

Angie and I talked easily about everything that came to our minds. We hit it off from the word "go." I could not imagine I could have been so fortunate. The girl I had admired just one year before was now the girl with whom I was sitting and conversing! What I didn't know is that God had a hand in what was about to take place.

As Angie said Goodnight, she invited me back. "We have family worship on Friday evening. Come and join us." I gladly agreed. I "floated" home, so excited about spending the evening with her that all I thought about until I saw her again was, seeing her again! The week seemed to drag by. We talked on the phone every day. Papa asked, "What do you have to talk about so much that you are on the phone every day?" I never had a good explanation, but I felt good about talking to her.

Finally Friday came. When I arrived, the house was filled with the aroma of food. Mrs. Marr invited me to have some dinner. Everyone was nice and so busy! With that many people living together, the house buzzed with activity. They also had a dog named Butch that growled when I came in. Angie quieted him and sent him to his closet to lie down. But Butch kept an eye on me. Angie said, "He'll bite you only if I tell him to."

After dinner we sat around and did the two things this family liked most—talking and laughing. The warm atmosphere helped me feel comfortable. Before long, someone said out loud, "Time for worship!" I had not heard that term in years. Family worship had disappeared from our home when Momma Haynes took sick.

We moved to the living room, where Bibles were passed out. But before we opened the Bibles, they sang songs. I felt somewhat awkward, because I had not been in such a setting for years. After someone offered prayer, they went around the room asking each person to read a text from the Bible. As my turn came nearer, my heart began to race. When someone said, "John, could you read the next verse?" I looked down at the open Bible on my lap, and I began to sweat. Droplets of perspiration fell to the pages. The others were amazed to see how reading the Bible affected me. I was so glad when my time to read had passed.

Angie quickly became more involved in my life. She asked a lot of questions: "John, did you grow up in the church?" "How is it that I had not seen you before?" "What was your mother like?" "What else do you do with your time?"

When she found out that I had grown up in the church, Angie felt free to give her opinions about what else I was doing. When she missed me at church, she asked where I was. I had to tell her that I was at a party. She could always tell me things I wouldn't listen to from adults. "John, you know that you should not be partying."

I knew she was right, but I excused it. "It's not that bad. At least, I still come to church sometimes."

Then Angie began showing up at my parties. I always wondered how she found out where it was. One Friday night, I was disc jockeying for a party that was held on the forty-fourth floor of the World Trade Center, in a club with windows that offered a 360-degree view of the city. I remember it as if it were yesterday. I was putting a record on the turntable, and when I looked up, Angie was standing there. "John," she said, you know you shouldn't be here. It's the Sabbath."

I said to her, "Yeah, I know, I know. Don't worry; I'll be at church tomorrow."

When she left, I felt out of place for the rest of the evening. In the back of my mind, I knew she was right, but I did not want to admit it. After all, I made more money playing music for a party than I made working all week. I didn't arrive home that night until after 4:00 a.m., too tired to go to church the next day.

I had friends whom I would occasionally party with. One of those friends was a guy named Hugh. He attended the same church as I did, and he partied just as I did. My friend Ricky owned a Datsun B210, and he rarely objected when I wanted to borrow it. One Friday evening, Hugh and I went to a party in Long Island, New York. It was like most parties I had attended—music, dancing, conversation, laughter, and drinking alcoholic beverages.

That night I had more to drink than I had anticipated. I did not feel drunk, because I did not lose composure. As I walked across the street when we left the club, I felt something hit my coattail. Then Hugh was beside me saying, "Didn't you hear me shouting for you to WATCH OUT!" A passing car I never saw had barely missed me. Looking back, I conclude that even though I was not where I was supposed to be, the Lord's grace still saved me from what could have happened. I don't believe in coincidence or luck. Only the Lord could have saved me, and He did.

I didn't think that partying was affecting me, either, but it was. I was more intoxicated by the lifestyle than I ever was by the alcohol. I was addicted to partying, immersed in the lifestyle in which I lived. My thoughts were consumed with how I could make the party better or where I could find the best party.

Dating Angie kept me in a battle zone. On one side, the Lord was using her to keep me convicted that my party lifestyle was wrong. On the other side, I was resisting the changes the Lord was trying to make in my life. There were times I even convinced her to go to places she would not have gone.

On my birthday, my sister and her boyfriend took Angie and me to a club in Bensonhurst, Brooklyn. It was the club where John Travolta's dance routine in *Saturday Night Fever* was filmed. Val had a surprise for me that night. The live band being featured was Archie Bell and the Drells. Before the show began, Val took me back stage to meet Archie Bell and the other band members. I was amazed—I didn't even know my sister knew the group. They were famous for their popular song "Tighten Up." That evening during their show, they played and sang "Happy Birthday" to me.

I want to be in a band like that, I thought. Before long, I bought an electric guitar and started a band with some of my neighborhood friends. When Angie invited me to camp meeting that summer, I opted out, because I had a concert to perform. It was becoming easier for me to say No to spiritual things and Yes to the things of the world. I thought I would be able to balance the two, but I found that there is no such thing as balance when it comes to choosing between the Lord and the world. The Bible says it this way, "No servant can serve two masters; for either he will hate the one and love the other, or else he will be loyal to the one and despise the other" (Luke 16:13, NKJV).

No kidding! Church began to get boring to me, and the world was getting more exciting. I grew up hearing "The world has nothing to offer." But as I went out in it, I found out that it had a lot to offer. Now I say to others, "It's not that the world has nothing to offer—it just depends on what you are looking for." If you are looking for the temporary, you can find it everywhere. If you are looking for the eternal, the world is, so to speak, "out of stock."

The world was coming at me fast and furious, and I was not trying to dodge it. I got to where I really didn't care to shield myself from the parties, pool hustling, and the nightlife of the city. New York had a lot to offer.

For a while, there was a tug-of-war between what Angie was trying to show me and what I wanted to do. Often when I did not show up in church, Angie would come to my house to get me. One Sabbath morning, I woke up hearing "pinging" sounds. Somehow I wasn't surprised to look out and find Angie throwing pebbles up at my window. When I tried to get her to leave, Papa opened the door for her. The next thing I knew, she was knocking on my room door. Instead of opening it, I kept telling her that I would meet her at church. To my surprise, Papa opened my room door and allowed her to come into my bedroom. Peering out from under my blanket, I watched while she looked in my wardrobe and took out clothes for me to wear to church. She waited downstairs until I was dressed, and then I walked to church with her. Although I didn't hear much of the sermon, I felt good to be there. Angie felt good that I was there too!

It was like the Lord had chosen me to be Angie's special project, because she would not leave me alone. Everywhere I went, she would find out about it or show up to bug me about being where I shouldn't be. Angie was kind of aggressive and shy at the same time. She was shy when it came to "boys," but she was aggressive when it came to church.

While we were dating, she said several times, "I'm not going to date anyone who's not going to go to church." I knew that she was serious, because she would not stop the cat-and-mouse game of making sure I was in church.

Adults tried to get me to stay in church, but they were not nearly as successful as Angie was. Of course, I had a personal interest in her and not in them. Angie realized her power over me, and she knew how to use it.

So Angie and I continued dating. Years passed, and after we finished high school, Angie went off to Oakwood College, in Huntsville, Alabama. I stayed in New York and worked. It was one of the loneliest times in my early adulthood. We still kept in touch by phone and letter. When I wrote her, I would draw colorful designs on the front of the envelope and then spray it with cologne. Whenever she got a letter, everyone in the dorm knew. It became the talk of Carter Hall. I still went to her home to visit her family. Her brothers were becoming like my brothers, especially Cliff and Ken, who were closest to my age. Lecia was like my sister for the same reason. Angie's mother, Aunt B., was like my mother.

When Angie came home for the summer, she invited me to their family worship on Friday evenings. She knew that if I was there, I wasn't likely to go to a party or to play billiards. She would see when I was fidgety and ask, "You want to go home, because you want to go out; am I right?" Even though I wouldn't outright admit it, she would get the answer out of me somehow. Angie had a twinkle in her eye that she would "turn on" to try to get to me. More times than not, she succeeded.

One Friday evening after family worship, Angie said, "I have a book that I want to give you." She handed me a book that I had vaguely heard of—*The Great Controversy*. This was about nine o'clock at night. As I thumbed through the book, one chapter title struck me as something I had heard much about over the years of attending church: "Prophecies Fulfilled." So I read that chapter. I was so engrossed that I couldn't stop with that one. I picked another chapter: "The Time of Trouble."

The Bible frightened me a little, but this book gripped me, and I could not put it down. I was hooked. All of a sudden it hit me: "Lord, I have been wasting my time. Please forgive me." I fell to the floor on my knees and leaned forward on the couch and wept as if a dam of emotions had broken.

Angie patted me on the back and said, "It's OK, John. I've been trying to tell you this for a long time."

When I got up off of my knees and sat back on the couch, I looked at Angie and said, "Do you realize how much time I've wasted? Do you realize how many people I've been leading astray? If I had only known this, I would not have been doing what I was doing."

I realized that I had to make some changes and that it would not be easy. It was almost midnight when Angie's brother Heaton asked if I needed a ride home. Before I left, I told Angie, "You can be sure that you will see me in church tomorrow." I took the book home with me and kept reading until I was too tired to keep my eyes open.

By this time, I was working at the Bank of America in the Wall Street area of downtown Manhattan. I had worked in various places in the downtown area. During my last year of high school, I worked on the twenty-second floor of Tower One of the World Trade Center. After I graduated, I worked for an insurance company where I actually got fired for refusing to work on Saturdays. Even with my partying, I could not work on the Sabbath day. The Lord—and His helper, Angie—were already working on my heart. With His help, I'm sure, I got a job at Chase Manhattan Bank, four blocks away, within a week.

I worked at Chase Manhattan Bank for almost a year before I changed jobs to work at Bank of America on 40 Broad Street. After my Friday-night encounter with *The Great Controversy*, Monday morning was different. I usually took my billiard cue and my big radio to work. But this Monday, I arrived at work with a Bible and *The Great Controversy*. I was so "on-fire" about what I had learned that I had to share it with somebody. What I didn't know was that another test was on its way.

I was sitting at my desk when the phone rang. It was an old church-and-party friend calling from Miami, Florida. She knew how popular I had become as a disc jockey. She said, "My family opened a disco in Miami, and they are looking for someone to be the disc jockey. They will start you off at $500 a week, they will pay your rent, and they will pay for you to move here. All you have to do is say Yes."

The devil wanted to circumvent what the Lord was about to do. The Lord could have kept me from getting the phone call. But now I understand that He wanted me to make some conscious decisions with all the facts on the table. I could answer my Miami friend with only "Give me some time to think about it."

After I hung up the phone, it was all too clear to me what the answer had to be. The very next day I called her back to say No. I faced other tests along the way. I had purchased hundreds of records over the years. I knew I needed to get rid of them and leave that life behind, but it was hard to do.

A guy at church asked me to play music for a party at his house. I wrestled for days with the question "Should I do it or should I not?" It was not until I saw him in church that I knew what my answer had to be. That Saturday, I went to his house and rang his doorbell. When he opened the door, he asked, "Where is your equipment? Where are your records?"

I looked at him and said, "I'm not playing for your party, and you better not ask me why, because you know better." Then I turned and went home.

Now I was determined to get rid of my records. But then I was asked to disc jockey for a wedding reception in the Bronx. The reception was for a friend of Angie's family, so I reasoned with myself, "OK, this is the last time." Watch out when you say, "This is my last time," because the devil will try to take your life and make sure that it is your last.

That weekend, Angie and I had rented a small Honda Civic to go to camp meeting. The wedding reception was later on Sunday, so we rushed home and folded down the back seat to pack the car full of sound equipment and records. It was raining as we rushed to the reception, and at Dekalb Avenue and Classon, the inevitable happened. The light turned red, and I pressed the brakes. But the car was so weighted down that it wouldn't stop skidding. We plowed right into the back of an Electra 225.

Angie was looking in the vanity mirror, and she did not have her seat belt fastened. On impact, her head broke the windshield. I bent the steering wheel and cracked my side of the windshield with my head. It was dreadful! Right then and there, I knew that if my life had ended, I would have been a lost man, because I was going against the Lord's will.

That evening I made up a list of my albums. I took the list with me to work on Monday morning to sell. Whatever I did not sell, I gave away. The people at my job knew that I had an extensive record collection, and it created a small frenzy when the news got out.

It was the strangest feeling to see my room empty of the records that had lined three walls of my room. I had spent years and thousands of dollars collecting them. But I needed to make a clean break from my past if I was going to follow God.

Angie was greatly supportive of these changes, naturally, since she was the one the Lord used to communicate to me that I needed to change. Later that summer, she invited me to go with her to some evangelistic meetings in Brooklyn. Pastor Lamar preached every night, and after attending for several weeks, we committed our lives to the Lord. At the end of the series, Angie and I were baptized together.

I never forgot the comment made by one of her brothers. He said, "They act like they're planning to get married." Although I did not have that thought immediately in my mind, time would prove that statement to be prophetic.

CHAPTER SIX

A New Beginning... Together

After working at Bank of America for two years, it was time for a change in my life. In January of 1979, Angie said, "John, you need to come with me to Oakwood College for Alumni Weekend. You haven't heard singing until you hear it at Oakwood!"

Oakwood College is about eight hundred miles from New York, but in April, Angie, her cousin Ronald, and I rented a yellow Ford Pinto hatchback and drove down. We got lost several times along the way, but when we arrived, I found that Oakwood was everything she said, and more.

The preaching and the singing captivated me. The Friday night sing-along and gospel concert, the Sabbath morning service with ten thousand worshipers at the Von Braun Civic Center, the evening concert at the radio station just off campus—it was like a taste of heaven. I heard, for the first time, Wintley Phipps and T. Marshall Kelly sing. We purchased Wintley Phipps' first album and played it much of the way home. I recorded as much of the festivities as I could, and I couldn't wait to get back and share it. By the time we got home, I was convinced I had to go back to Oakwood College and enroll as a student.

Angie and I devised a plan to go back to Oakwood together. Since I needed money to get enrolled, I sat down with Papa and his new wife, Edna, and asked them for financial support. But Papa wasn't convinced. He had money, but because of his life of difficulty and hard work, he held on to it. After much pleading, he finally agreed to give me the enrollment fee and some money to get me settled.

My first trip in an airplane was to enroll at Oakwood in 1979. Enrolling wasn't as easy as I had thought, but after three days in lines filling out forms, I finally got settled in. During the next few wonderful months, Angie and I spent a lot of time together with the Lord. If I could have imagined the Lord's wonderful plans for my life, I would have given up the music of the world years sooner. I had thought that serving God was limiting and therefore boring. Church seemed like the place where square people attended and where rules and regulations were imposed. However, when I surrendered my will to the Lord, I found out that the world was imposing its values on me while the Lord was trying to show me the better and easier way of life. From outside the church, my views of a Christian life were distorted. From inside, my views were clear.

I thought I would find "a future" and "a hope" in Manhattan. What I did not know was that there is no future and no hope unless the Lord is the center of my life. It was difficult to see, because the world was blocking my view of the Lord. It was almost impossible to understand, because the noise of the world's music kept me from hearing the voice of the Holy Spirit. When I heard people in church talk about how "wonderful" the Lord was to them, it sounded as "flowery nonsense" to me, because my mind was so clogged with my own ideas of "wonderful." As much as I tried to see what the Christian life would be like, I really did not understand it until I became a Christian.

To me, being a non-Christian is like putting on a bathing suit on a 100-degree day and then walking around the edges of a beautiful pool wondering why the people in the water are so exuberant and happy. I did not know true life until I knew the Lord.

A NEW BEGINNING . . . TOGETHER

So many times we feel we need to remedy our situation before we can come to the Lord in prayer. What we don't realize is that the Lord knows more about us than we are willing to admit about ourselves. We fool ourselves into thinking we need to clean up ourselves *before* we come to the Lord. In reality, there is no such thing as being clean unless we have the Lord in our lives.

At Oakwood College I learned that the Lord was my friend, not because I fit all of the parameters of righteousness but because of His love for me. I knew there were things in my life that still needed to be changed. However, when I heard the minister say things like "Jesus loves you as you are," I felt encouraged. I later found out that although He does love us just as we are, it is also true that His love is too great to leave us in the condition He finds us.

Being away from home was also a type of cleansing for me. The city was a constant reminder of things that were unclean: the streets, the nightlife, the entertainment, the crime, and the noise. When I lived in Brooklyn, I was held up at gunpoint twice. Both times I was so angry afterward that I went looking for the perpetrators to take back what was mine. But once again, the Lord delivered me from a couple of situations that could have landed me in jail or cost me my life.

Near the end of my first term at Oakwood, I called home to "collect" on a promise that Papa had made to me before I left. He had promised to help me buy a reasonably priced used car that I could use as I worked my way through school. That day I was so excited about staying at Oakwood that the phone call couldn't happen soon enough.

I still don't know what happened after I left, but Papa had changed his mind. He said, "It was your idea to go away to school, not mine. All I'm sending you is a one-way plane ticket to come home! I'm not wasting my money on you!"

I tried my best to convince him, but his mind was made up. I was crushed. I asked the school if there was any way to work out finances so that I could stay, but their answer was also No. Two weeks later, the school term was up, and I returned home. I took a cab home from the airport, back to the same room I had left. Papa met me with a subdued "Welcome home," and the subject of my education was never discussed.

The next week, I went back to downtown Manhattan, found a job, and immersed myself in the working world. After considering several options, I chose to pursue an associate degree in electronics at the Albert Merrill School. I worked all day and went to school in the evenings as I successfully completed the courses.

But I didn't give up on a car. Before many months went by, I said, "Papa, you're not getting any younger, and the neighborhood is not getting any safer. If you buy me a car, I can take you wherever you want to go." I don't know if I was more persuasive than before or what, but Papa shocked me by asking how much I would need. Then he gave me $1,000 toward a used car. I found a 1976 Toyota Corona station wagon with approximately seventy thousand miles on it that seemed just right.

Just as promised, Papa and I used the car together quite often. He even took a trip up to camp meeting with Angie and her mother and me. This was the first time he agreed to go to Victory Lake, knowing that it was a church-sponsored, preaching-and-singing event. After the morning services, we got together with Angie's large family, including cousins, aunts, and uncles and enjoyed our lunch. It was one of my most memorable times with Papa, and I thanked him again for helping me buy a car.

I was still working downtown at Chemical Bank, and they asked for something I didn't have—a copy of my birth certificate. It seemed like a strange request, but I filed the paperwork to ask for it. When it arrived, I was in for the shock of my life!

I had always wondered about my parents. Even when my natural father returned in 1971, I had learned very little about my mother. So my birth certificate had information I had never seen before. My sister had always said she thought we had a brother. The birth certificate indicated this—that my mother had given birth to two children before me. I also found out much more about my mother. Her place of birth was listed as St. Thomas, Unites States Virgin Islands. Her address, at the time of my birth, was also listed: 128 West 70 Street, Manhattan. Most important of all, it gave my mother's complete name: Rosario Maria Lomacang. When we were younger, Val always told me that our mother's name was Kim and that she looked Asian.

I was so excited to find out these things that I called Angie and asked her to go with me to my mother's old address. She agreed, and I thought the workday would never end. When we finally stood on 70 Street, I stopped and looked around. *This is where I lived when I was born*, I thought. As we walked up to 128 West 70, I thought, *My real mother walked on these steps.*

I rang the doorbell and waited anxiously. Finally, the inside lock clicked, and a little man opened the door. Obviously, I didn't know him, but that didn't faze me. "Do you know if a lady lived here named Rosario Lomacang or Maria Lomacang or Kim?"

"How long ago are you talking about?" he asked.

"About twenty-six years."

"Twenty-six years!" He shook his head. "How do you expect me to remember who lived here twenty-six years ago? I didn't even live here twenty-six years ago. I've been here about ten years, and I've never heard the name in all that time. Sorry I couldn't be of more help to you."

Just before he closed the door, I asked, "Is there anyone else here who may know?"

He said, "No one else has lived here as long as I have. I work for the landlord, and I'm the building super!"

Angie looked at me sadly. "Oh well," she said, "what do you do now?"

We walked away slowly. I could only answer, "I don't have any idea what to do now. I guess I'll just hold onto this birth certificate. Maybe it will come in handy in the future."

When I showed the birth certificate to my sister, Val, she asked,

"Where's the information about Johnny?" There was no information about my father. That part of the certificate was blank.

Time passed. Angie and I continued dating. So much had happened in the nine years that we had known each other. We dated, then broke up, and then resumed dating. Her brother Heaton was usually pushing us one direction or the other. Sometimes he tried to get rid of me; other times he was my good friend. Over the years, he would periodically ask me my intentions concerning his sister. He would ask, "How long do you plan to date Angie?"

My usual answer was "I don't know." There were times I thought that he was trying to get me to quit dating his sister. Most of the time, I would listen to his rant and rave and then just go about my business. However, in April 1983, his speech was a little different.

Heaton said, "You've been dating my sister for about nine years. You need to make up your mind soon. Are you going to marry her or not?"

"I am going to marry her!" I answered.

Then he looked me in the eye and asked, "When?"

I was taken aback by the intensity of his question. In a rush, I said, "What about next month!"

He was shocked into silence! Finally he said, "I hope you're serious." Looking back, I must conclude that a little encouragement never hurt anyone.

That evening I shared my decision with Angie and her mother. They were shocked too. Angie said, "John, you're supposed to ask me to marry you! My brother isn't supposed to ask you to marry me!"

Then I went home and told Papa and Val. They were shocked. "When?" Papa asked.

"One month from now," I announced. The next Sunday evening, Angie, her mother, Papa, and I got together at Angie's house to plan. It was amazing to see how quickly it could all happen. In one short month we secured the hall, the church, the pastor, the musicians, the groom's men, the bridesmaids, and the food. We had the bridesmaids' dresses handmade, had the cake homemade, sent out the invitations, made phone calls, and planned our honeymoon. We had no time to get nervous and no time to think twice about our decision. When the planning was completed, the wedding was only a week away.

The wedding was to be held at Bethel, my home church. Pastor E. T. Mimms was going to officiate. Angie's cousin, Mrs. Chollette, made the wedding cake—a West Indian fruitcake traditionally called a "Black Cake."

The day finally arrived, and people came from everywhere—about four hundred of them. I really didn't feel any different. I dressed by myself and met the groom's men at the church. My best man was my long-time friend Ricky.

The wedding was supposed to start at 2:00 p.m., but it didn't. Angie did what most brides should not do on their wedding day—she went to get her hair done. And everything that could go wrong did. The people at church were growing restless, and so was the pastor. I tried to remain calm, so everyone else would be encouraged. Finally, after almost two hours, Angie arrived—in a Ford Mustang instead of the antique Bentley in which her brother-in-law had planned to chauffeur her.

When we heard the cry, "She's here. The bride is here!" Ricky looked at me and said, "Too late to turn back now! Are you nervous?"

I was a little nervous, but after all, I had known Angie for nine years. I thought, *What makes today any different? I know it's my wedding day. I'll be all right.* I was fine standing on the platform with the pastor, looking out at the sea of faces. But having a large wedding is an experience like no other. I watched the bridesmaids and groomsmen make their way down the aisle, but somehow the bridal march snuck up on me. Suddenly, I saw Angie at the back of the church, covered in white lace. As she began to make her way down the aisle, I could not believe the feeling that came over me. I had seen her before, but never before had she looked so breathtakingly beautiful. In a very soft voice, I said, "Wow!"

At that moment, it all struck me. This was the church where I was raised. This was where Mrs. Haynes had taught me about the Lord. This is where the Lord had waited patiently to shape me and mold me for His glory. Only having Momma Haynes there could have made the moment more complete. Tears came to my eyes as I saw Papa standing there with a smile of satisfaction on his face. Mrs. Marr looked up the aisle as her daughter held onto the arm of her oldest brother, Lance.

The pastor broke into my thoughts with the question, "Who gives this woman to be married to this man?" Lance proudly responded, "I do!" As he escorted my bride to my side, I glanced through her lace veil and saw her cheeks being caressed by tears of joy. She smiled and winked at me, and we held onto each other's hand even more tightly. The ride of our lives was about to begin.

The ceremony went smoothly after the late start. I surprised everyone by singing the song "For Baby" to Angie. Sniffles and smiles spread around the sanctuary. No song I had ever sung brought me as much joy as singing to my bride that day. I began to understand a small part of what the Lord must feel about His church. Nothing and no one had my undivided attention like my beautiful bride did that day.

Pastor Mimms instructed us to hold each other's hand and repeat after him. I couldn't say "I do" fast enough. Angie seconded my decision with her "I do." At that declaration, the pastor said, "I now pronounce you man and wife. You may kiss your bride." With one sweet kiss, we began our life together. I barely understood it that day, but Angie was just the person the Lord had chosen for me. She would prove to be the link to the unfolding of events that would change my life forever.

That evening, we were so anxious to go on our honeymoon that we threw some clothes into a suitcase and set off to Atlantic City, New Jersey. But we were so tired that we only drove a few miles before we pulled over at a tollbooth and slept until the sun rose. When we finally made our way to the hotel, someone I knew was working the desk. She

A NEW BEGINNING . . . TOGETHER

upgraded our room to an ocean-view suite. The Lord showed us from the beginning that our lives would be filled with one blessing after another.

After we left our honeymoon suite, we hit the road and drove south. Our final destination was Orlando, Florida. We stopped along the way to visit one family member after another until we made it to Angie's Aunt Sissy's house. All along the way, Angie talked about moving to Florida, but I just couldn't see making that move anytime soon.

But Angie was so convinced that she talked me into opening a bank account in Orlando, where we deposited the money we had been given at the wedding. Angie said, "This way we will have some money when we come back."

Everyone we talked to agreed that moving to Florida was a great idea. It almost seemed like a conspiracy. All the way back to New York, Angie talked about Florida and our future.

CHAPTER SEVEN

Taking Off

We arrived home to stare reality in the face. Instead of a nice apartment to begin our new life together, we had a single room, my bedroom—the same room I lived in while we were dating. We shared a bathroom with two other tenants and a kitchen with a total of five other tenants. Angie looked at me without saying a word, but I could see it in her eyes: "Can you understand why I want to move to Florida?"

But Angie smiled and made the best of it. She never complained. She knew it was just temporary. After just a few weeks, we began looking for an apartment. We found several places that would be ideal, but the rent was high. The more we looked, the more we realized that something had to give, and soon.

By this time, three months had passed since the wedding, and we still hadn't even seen the wedding photo proofs. After calling the photographer repeatedly with no results, we finally went to his shop in Queens and picked up our pictures. About a week later, we decided at the last minute to go with a church group on a weekend outing to North Carolina. We left the car parked in front of the church, sure that it would be safe there. If a car can't be safe in front of a church, where can it be safe?

TAKING OFF

We returned to find the car had been broken into and everything inside stolen—including our wedding photos. We were so upset that we said to each other, "That's it! We're leaving New York! Who wants to be a part of a city where even personal wedding photos are not safe?"

To make matters worse, our photographer had no backup negatives for our wedding pictures. They were gone forever. That did it. We were determined to leave the city of New York and move to Orlando.

Over the years, when Papa and I had disagreements, he would sometimes say, "If you don't like it, you can leave!" I would always respond, "I'm not leaving until I'm married!" Well, the day had finally arrived—I was leaving.

The day we left was heart-wrenching for me. I was about to leave "home," the place I had lived all my life. Even more important, I was about to leave Papa. We packed everything into Angie's cousin Richie's van (he was moving to Florida also), and I went back into the house to take one last look at my bedroom. Papa walked slowly up the stairs behind me, looking more sober than usual. He was wearing sunshades and had a towel over one shoulder. He didn't look at me, he just asked in a soft trembling voice, "Junior, are you done packing?"

"Yes, Papa," I answered.

"So are you ready to leave now?"

Again I answered softly, "Yes, Papa. Angie and Richie are waiting for me downstairs." He turned his back, picked up the end of his towel, and lightly nudged his sunshades as he wiped his face. I couldn't remember the last time I saw Papa shed a tear. That show of emotion made it clear to me that his hard exterior was just a front. Under it all, he was the same loving and caring man who put his life on pause to make room for me twenty-five years ago. He was the only father I knew for thirteen years. Even after my natural father appeared, Papa was still the one who stood by my side through thick and thin.

I gently put my arms around him. "Papa, I feel the same way."

He said, "I'm going to miss you. Are you going to call me when you get to Florida?"

"Papa, you know that I will. I'm going to miss you too." We talked for a few minutes about the good times, and then I asked him to pray with me. Turning to walk away was so hard. I felt as if I was abandoning him. I wanted to stay, but I knew the time had come to go. It was time to put into practice the things he had taught me. He taught me the value of independence, and now it was time to be independent. Papa followed me down the stairs and out into the front yard, where Angie and I bade him farewell, got into the car, and drove off slowly until he was out of our view.

With every possession we owned, we began our journey south. Because of stops to visit family, it was late on the evening of the second day when we pulled up into the driveway of Angie's Aunt Sissy. She had invited us to stay at her house, in a large remodeled room that was formerly the garage. Aunt Sissy was doing what she had done for so many others, opening her heart and home.

Aunt Sissy was one of a kind. One of her mysteries was her age—no one knew it, and she wasn't telling. Angie's mother was her youngest sister. Living with her was like living with a female version of Papa. She was very wise, and she often spoke her mind. On the other hand, Aunt Sissy was a blast to be around. She got along well with anyone, as long as they agreed to do things her way.

Aunt Sissy was also a trooper for the church. To this day, I have a Bible that she gave to me. As soon as we moved in, she made sure we became members at her church. She invited her pastor over to visit with us, and in no time at all, we were attending the Altamonte Springs Seventh-day Adventist Church.

Florida was not an easy place for us to establish ourselves. Even though it was September, it was still very hot and very humid in Orlando. Angie and I went out every day searching for employment, but everywhere we went, the doors were difficult to open. Aunt Sissy wasn't offering a free ride—she needed the financial support. The savings account we had opened during our honeymoon was shrinking rapidly. Nothing was coming in—everything was going out. It became scary to go to the bank.

We began to wonder why we had moved to Florida, to wonder if we had jumped ahead of God's plan for us. Finally one evening, after a long day of job searching, we stopped by the bank, but there was not enough money left in the account to make a withdrawal. After a silent ride back to Aunt Sissy's, we parked in front of the house and looked at each other. "Let's pray," I suggested. There were job interviews with replies pending, and we were at the end of our rope. We needed an answer from the Lord.

As we were ending the prayer, Aunt Sissy came to the front door and called out, "Angie, there is a phone call for you." The phone call was a job offer beginning the following Monday. To say that we thanked and praised the Lord is an understatement. It was just like the Bible promise says: " 'It shall come to pass that before they call, I will answer; and while they are still speaking, I will hear' " (Isaiah 65:24, NKJV).

But no matter where I applied, I just couldn't seem to find a job. It began to hurt my self-esteem. It got harder every day to go out and look again. Although people at church asked how my job search was going, none of them offered to help. I started to doubt their sincerity about my welfare. What I didn't know was that the Lord had completely different plans for me.

When you don't know the Lord's plans for your life, you can begin to blame people rather than being patient. One of the greatest lessons the Lord wanted me to learn was patience. I wanted a job immediately, and the kind of job I wanted was not in the Lord's plan.

To fill my time after I came home from the endless job interviews, I found some musical accompaniment background tracks and prepared to sing when I was asked. Before long, I was singing at various churches, at weddings, and even giving complete concerts. Two friends, Ruth and Jack, joined me in this singing ministry. We would periodically meet and give concerts together.

In January 1984, I was asked to give a concert in Melbourne, Florida, at Jack's home church. That same weekend, Angie's mother bought tickets to the Heritage Singers' concert to be held at the Tupperware Auditorium, in Kissimmee. Mrs. Marr said, "John, you and Angie have to come to the concert."

I replied, "I already have a concert the same night, so I cannot come."

She insisted. "I paid for tickets for you and Angie, and you have to come, even if you come for just half of the concert."

"Mrs. Marr, Melbourne is seventy miles from there. There's no way that we are going to be able to make it for the concert." She kept insisting. I wondered why she was so persistent, because it was out of character for her. To end the dispute, I said, "OK, we'll be there, but we may miss most of the concert."

We got to the Melbourne church early and set up for the concert. In the back of my mind, I could hear Angie's mother say, "I'll be looking for you." Angie was my soundperson. She mixed the music and the microphones while I sang. It was a good concert, but I couldn't forget our appointment with her mother that evening. I didn't want to disappoint her, so as soon as my concert was finished, we shook hands cordially but as quickly as possible.

The tickets were at the front door of the concert hall, just as Angie's mother had promised. As we walked in, it was a pleasure to hear the Heritage Singers again. They had long been one of my favorite Christian singing groups. To our surprise, Angie's mother had reserved seats for us next to her, just a few rows from the stage. The group sang one more song, and then Max Mace announced that they were going to have a brief intermission before the second half began.

The half-time artist was Clifton Davis, a man who had become famous for starring on the television comedy "That's My Momma." He had come back to the church after leaving show business, and he was now singing to the glory of the Lord. Near the end of the concert, Monty Jackson and Jackie Leiske sang a song that I had been singing with a girl named Maureen—"More Than Wonderful." During that song, one of the members from my church said to me, "John, you should be up there. You can sing just as good as they can."

When the concert was ending, Max Mace announced that they were looking for a second tenor to join the group in July of that year. Angie looked at me. I looked at her. Without a word being spoken, she knew what I was thinking. Max had mentioned that there would be auditions after the concert for those who were interested. I was interested, all right. Just having given a concert, my voice was still warm and ready to go.

"What song would you sing to audition?" Angie asked.

"I'll sing a song that Heritage is familiar with," I decided. "I'll do 'He Died of a Broken Heart.' " I gave the sound track to the soundman, Greg Mace, Max's son, then went to the stage where Max gave me the microphone. The rest of the group was walking all around me, taking down the sound system. When I began to sing, they stopped to listen. I was somewhat surprised, because I knew how good they were. Afterward some of them said to me, "That was very good," and shook my hand.

Max Mace asked for my phone number and address. He said, "We will be in touch with you soon."

I thought to myself, *Good try, but that sounded like another "don't call us, we'll call you" statement.*

Clifton Davis came over and said, "That was good. You have a nice voice." Angie and I talked with him for a little while and then turned to head out.

I didn't think that I would hear from Max, so I just settled for the excitement of singing for them that night. But on our way out, Max stopped me again. "We finish our summer tour in July. I'll be in touch soon." I couldn't help but feel excited—he looked so interested in me when he said that. All the way home I couldn't help talking about the possibility of singing with the Heritage Singers.

After that experience, I stopped complaining about not being able to find a job and did something about it. I got involved in more of the church activities, leading out whenever possible. Some of the smaller churches in the greater Orlando area invited me to preach. I was also allowed to lead out in a Friday-night study group, mostly for youth. Friday nights at Aunt Sissy's house became the place to be, and our room was packed as we sang and studied together.

One young man who joined us went on to make his mark in secular music—Brian McKnight. He and I often played basketball with his brother Claude McKnight, who is a member of the famous six-part harmony male group, Take 6. Brian often told me, "John, I'm not going to sing unless you run the sound." To this day, Brian and Claude's mother, Elaine, is a close friend of Angie's eldest sister, Elaine.

During this time, I made friends with a number of people who impacted my life in significant ways. Shortly before I had a chance to audition for the Heritage Singers, I met Maureen Mair, and we began to sing together. One Sabbath afternoon, we were invited to sing for the well-known prison ministry "Jesus Behind Bars." Its founder, David Mould, invited Maureen and me to sing at a rally at the Mount Sinai SDA Church, in downtown Orlando. We sang a song that was made famous by Larnell Harris and Sandi Patti, "More Than Wonderful." It went so well that David Mould asked me to work for him.

The very next week I was hired as one of the junior accountants for his ministry. I worked in the same office as Robert Thompson, the main accountant for the company. I was so excited to be working for a Christian organization that allowed me to end work early every Friday. I was also getting more opportunities to travel and sing.

I was also invited to travel to the West Coast with "Jesus Behind Bars." David Mould assembled a team to go to a maximum security state prison in Soledad, California. To my surprise, one of the persons on the team was Clifton Davis, whom I had met at the Heritage Singers concert. Ron Halverson, a well-known preacher who had been a member of gangs years before in Brooklyn, New York, joined us, as well as Maureen and another lady named Marta Zintel.

What I did not know was that God was about to catapult me into the public arena. He was about to make me visible, both for His glory and to do something remarkable for me personally. One evening that June, a friend called to tell me about a Christian music talent search being held locally. By then, there was only one day left to enter. I was the last of more than one hundred contestants as I entered a song Maureen and I had recorded.

By this time, I had given up hoping to hear from the Heritage Singers. I was sure they had selected some other singer. But one day after the phone rang, Aunt Sissy called out, "John, there's a man on the phone who says that his name is Max."

I grabbed the phone, trying to act as though I wasn't anxious. "Hi, Mr. Mace," I said.

"Call me Max," he insisted. "Are you still interested in singing with us?"

"I sure am!"

He went on, "I would have called you sooner, but I lost my contact information for you. I practically tore up my desk looking for it. I apologize for taking so long."

I was not about to complain. Max said, "What I would like you to do is send me some of your songs on tape. Express them to me here in Seattle." I couldn't believe he was still interested in me. I looked at Angie to give her a hint of what was happening, and then I took the information from him.

The very next day I recorded some songs and sent them to him. About a week later, Max called again. "I would like to hear you sing some songs in a little different style," he said.

I sent Max a song I had recorded before I left New York called "Two Sides of You." My friend Peter Gibbs wrote it, and I sang it with him and his wife, Delissa. A week passed before Max called again. This time I could hear the smile in his voice. "John, if you're still interested in singing with us, I would like to extend the opportunity to you to join us."

If you had seen my face, you would have thought I was about to burst with joy. I tried to motion to Angie that Max was asking me to join the group as I answered "Of course I'm interested in joining the Heritage Singers!"

Max went on. "This September, we'll be taking a nine-country tour of Europe."

My eyes lighted up. Angie kept whispering to me, "What's he saying? Tell me!"

All of a sudden I realized that his invitation hadn't included anything about my wife. "Mr. Mace, I am married, so I could only join you if my wife can come with me."

Max set my mind at ease. "We wouldn't even think of asking you not to bring her," he said. "We can find something for her to do. I'll talk to my wife, and maybe we can hire her to be our on-the-road bookkeeper."

I was so excited that I had to ask him to hold for a moment so I could explain it all to Angie. By this time, her mother had heard the commotion. "What's happening?" she asked. I told her we were being invited to join the Heritage Singers, and we did not know whether to accept it or not. Angie and I looked at Mrs. Marr as if we were waiting for some direction. She said, "Opportunity only knocks once! GO!"

I put the phone to my ear and said, "Max, we have decided to accept your offer. Thanks so much for remembering us."

He said, "Don't thank me; thank my son Greg—he remembered you." Before our conversation ended, the ball was rolling. Max told us we needed to be in California some time in July and that his wife, Lucy, would send us the details.

All of a sudden, it seemed as if our lives were taking off. There were so many things to do to get ready to go to California. And we didn't even know how we were going to get there. We would have to drive, but our car was too old to survive a 3,000-mile drive.

A few days later, I was driving my car to work when the engine began to make funny sounds. I took it to a Christian mechanic named Jay. "How much would you charge to fix my car?" I asked.

"That depends," he answered. "What's wrong with it?" I explained that it sounded like a chain was rubbing in the engine. "That sounds like the timing chain tension mechanism is stuck," he decided. "That would cost about $1,000 to fix."

"Ouch!" I said. "Why so expensive?" He explained that it was nearly as much work as rebuilding the engine. "Jay, my car is not even worth $1,000. Even if it was, I don't have that kind of money." Then I had a bright idea. "I'm going to have to rebuild the engine myself!"

He looked at me. "Have you ever rebuilt an engine?"

I could only answer "No, but I could buy the book and follow the instructions."

He looked at me as if I were crazy. "If you don't know what you're doing, the engine will blow up in your face."

Crazy or not, I had no alternatives. I called a friend and asked if I could use his garage to store my car while I rebuilt the engine. He offered to help me and offered the use of his motorcycle while we worked on the car.

I bought the *Chilton's Auto Manual* for a 1976 Toyota Corona station wagon. I must admit, it looked like a foreign language to me. But if we planned to go to California, that car was our only way there.

Robert and I took the engine apart piece by piece. We read the instructions carefully as we went. It was far more difficult than we had anticipated. Finally, we had the engine all apart and many of the parts labeled, so we'd know where they went. Angie stopped by, took one look, and asked, "What have you gotten yourself into?"

Robert and I looked at each other and burst into laughter. I said, "We don't know what we're doing. We just hope the instructions in the book are correct!"

I couldn't help but think about the Bible and see how following it had led me to where I was. It was just that simple—read it and follow the instructions. I had simple faith, and as I took inventory of where I was, I concluded, "I got here by reading the Bible and following it." It was the same with rebuilding the engine. I was not a mechanic. My degree in electronics helped me understand the importance of following detailed instructions.

So much was happening in our lives at the same time. The talent search was going on, and we were packing to leave for California in a few short weeks. Besides that, Max Mace had arranged for me to take a short three-day trip to California to record a song for a new Heritage Singers' album. The short trip also would allow me to take some clothes by plane, leaving less for Angie and me to take as we drove.

What else could possibly happen in one month, I wondered. But the most unexpected thing of all was just around the corner.

CHAPTER EIGHT

More Than Wonderful

I was riding Robert's motorcycle to work and borrowing Aunt Sissy's car to drive to the talent-contest events in the evening. Just before I left for California to record with Heritage, Maureen and I found out that we made it past the first round in the talent search. There would be one more contest before the finals.

For the semifinals, we stayed with the same two songs, "More Than Wonderful" and "When the Time Comes." God worked it out so we were among the top ten finalists. Along with the other finalists, our names were announced on local radio station WAJL.

When I arrived at work—on motorcycle—one of my co-workers told me about hearing my name on the radio, following the semifinals. Others were hearing my name, as well, as I found out later that afternoon.

Another lady was listening to the same Christian radio station through an earphone as she worked. Every hour, on the hour, the names of the last ten contestants were mentioned, along with an invitation to attend the final talent contest.

The name "John Lomacang" immediately got her attention. She thought, *Did I hear them say Lomacang? Not likely,* she concluded. It would be too much of a coincidence. An hour later, the name was mentioned again: "John Lomacang."

This time she was sure. "They did say Lomacang—John Lomacang!" She reached for the phone and quickly called the radio station. "Was someone named 'Lomacang' mentioned just a few minutes ago on your station?"

"Yes," the station secretary replied. "He's one of the talent-search finalists."

"Can you tell me something about him?" the caller asked.

The secretary said, "Well, he's tall, and he's probably Spanish." Before going any further, the secretary asked, "Can you please give me your name?"

"My name is Teresa Milner," the caller stated. "Can you give me his phone number?"

"No, I cannot. But if you give me your name and number, I will see that he gets a message."

Teresa left the message and waited.

It was about 10:15 a.m. on Friday morning, June 22, 1984. I was finishing up some work when I was paged over the intercom: "John, there is a call for you on line 2."

I picked up the phone. "Hello, this is John. How can I help you?"

"Hello, John," said a voice I didn't recognize. "I received a phone call from a lady who thinks that you and she may be related. She left her phone number and wants you to call her." I knew better than that. "Who is this?" I asked. "Is this some kind of joke?"

The woman on the phone laughed. "This is not a hoax. I am the secretary at WAJL, the station that sponsored the talent search!"

I finally thanked her then hung up and dialed the number she had given me. When a woman answered, I introduced myself. She said, "Hello. My name is Teresa; we've never met, but I wanted to speak to you. When I heard your name on the radio today, it surprised me."

"Why would my name surprise you?" I asked.

Her answer set my pulse racing. "I think we might be related. My maiden name was also Lomacang."

I had never met anyone who shared the same name as my sister and me. "Please, tell me more," I asked.

She began her story. "When I was being raised in the Virgin Islands, my father was a fisherman. The islanders were jealous of him and his friend, because they were not natives of St. Thomas."

I could hardly believe what I was hearing. My statistical birth certificate listed St. Thomas, US Virgin Islands, as the place where my mother was born. I didn't interrupt Teresa; I tried to remain calm, but inside, my emotions were running wild.

She continued: "Let me take you back a little farther. My father was born in the Philippines. He was a sailor on a ship that was on its way back to the Philippines. But he took sick, and since they were passing through the islands, he was admitted into a hospital on St. Thomas."

This seemed like a far-fetched way of explaining, but I just listened and held my breath. My body was at my desk, but my mind was on hold. All I could see was Robert across the room, looking at me with great concern. Before she went any further, I asked, "What was your name again?"

"Teresa," she reminded me, and then, in the same breath, she continued the story. "While he was in the hospital, he was cared for by a French nursing student named Inger. Before long, they fell in love and got married. They settled in a small town called French Town. Another man from the Philippines lived there, and they became good friends and fishing buddies. My father's boat was large enough to sail to the mainland of the United States."

I broke in with a question. "What do I have to do with you and your father? I'm not from the Virgin Islands."

"Let me explain," she said. "My father disappeared shortly before my second sister was born. We're not sure what happened to him. Some said he and his friend left the islands and went to Miami. But there was a rumor that he had been killed at sea."

She went on. "I have always looked for some sign that our father was still alive. So, when I heard your name on the radio, I thought there must be some connection. When I found out that your last name and my maiden name are spelled the same, I thought that maybe you were from his new family, that maybe we were related. That spelling is so rare."

Then she had some questions for me. "Tell me a little about yourself. Where are you from?"

"I was born and raised in New York," I answered. "I have a sister named Vivian and a niece named Tiashia. They still live in New York. I have a wife named Angela—I call her Angie. We've been married a little more than a year."

She interrupted me. "That's strange!"

I thought, *What's strange? What does she mean?*

She asked, "Did you say that you have a sister named Vivian?" I said Yes. Then she said something that made my pulse race. "I have a sister who said she had a daughter named Vivian and a son named John, but we didn't believe her, because she couldn't produce any evidence!"

The next question she asked me almost killed me.

"By any chance, is your mother's name Rosario?"

I took a deep breath to catch my composure and said, "Yes it is! It's Rosario Maria Lomacang!" By this time I was about to lose it. I could hardly catch my breath; I was hyperventilating.

"That's my sister!" she cried.

I immediately yelled, "IS SHE ALIVE? IS SHE ALIVE?" Then I dropped the phone and began crying uncontrollably. Robert stared at me and began asking, "What's wrong? What's going on? Who's on the phone?"

I couldn't even answer him. I grabbed the phone from the desk and began yelling again, "IS SHE ALIVE? IS SHE ALIVE? Tell me, IS SHE ALIVE?"

Teresa was trying to answer. "YES, she's alive, and she's living in the Virgin Islands!" She listened to my sobs and spoke with tears in her voice. "I need to see you today! When I see you, I will know whether or not you're Rosie's son. Can you come to my job right away?"

I agreed. She told me where to meet her. Immediately I called Angie at her job. I had every intention of telling her what was happening, but I couldn't even get it out. It was all I could do to catch my breath and keep repeating, "Something wonderful happened! Something great happened!"

"What are you talking about?" Angie asked. "What happened?"

I couldn't explain anything, because I couldn't gather my thoughts. I finally said, "Meet me in the lobby at your work!" She agreed.

After I hung up the phone, I went into shock. I began walking around the office crying and repeating, "She's alive! She's alive! She's alive!" I walked past the receptionist desk in the lobby and kept repeating the same thing. The receptionist was a good friend of mine named Evol. I walked up to her crying and saying, "She's alive! She's alive! She's alive!"

Evol could only ask, "John! What do you mean? What do you mean she's alive? Who is she?"

I took another deep breath and mustered up enough energy to get out the answer: "MY MOTHER IS ALIVE!" As soon as I said it, I slumped over her desk and continued crying. By then practically the whole office staff was in the lobby, watching what was unfolding.

Since I could hardly stand up, I was in no shape to ride a motorcycle. I pleaded with Evol, "Please take me to Angie! Please?" She hustled me into her car, and we took off. When we finally arrived, Angie was waiting for me in the lobby.

Angie saw me crying and ran toward me asking, "What happened?"

All I could say was "She's alive! She's alive! She's alive!"

"Who's alive?" Angie demanded.

Finally I got the words out. "My mother! My mother is alive! You have to come with me now. I have to go to meet this woman at her job; I'll explain it on the way."

Angie explained to her supervisor, and then we went home to change instead of going straight to meet Teresa. We were so nervous that we weren't thinking clearly. We had already been nicely dressed for work. On the way, Angie said, "When you called, I didn't know what had happened. After I hung up, someone asked me what was going on. I told them that you said 'Something great happened.' When they asked me what I thought that you meant, I said 'Maybe he hit the lottery!'"

I couldn't help laughing. "Hit the lottery! I don't even play the lottery! What made you think that?"

About twenty minutes later, we arrived at The Hartford Insurance Company, where Teresa worked. But I had been so caught up in our conversation earlier that I forgot to ask Teresa her last name. At the front desk, I simply said, "I would like to speak to Teresa."

The receptionist said, "There are three Teresas here. Which one would you like to speak to?"

I had to say "I don't know which one!"

The receptionist asked, "What does she look like?" Again I had no answer—I had never seen this woman.

It took a few minutes to find her, but eventually they did. Angie and I waited in the foyer, at the entrance of an office area. When I saw Teresa, I was surprised. She was very fair-skinned, almost Caucasian looking. She was quite different in complexion from the people that raised me.

Angie and I just stood there as she walked slowly toward us with a questioning glaze on her face. She stopped close enough in front of me to reach out and take hold of my hands. Looking intently in my face, she squeezed my hands and said, "Yes, you're Rosie's son. I can see it in your face."

Teresa hugged me and began to cry. I began to cry. Angie began to cry. Her supervisor called, "Terry, go to lunch. Take all the time you need, just go to lunch."

Teresa led me by the hand to their cafeteria. It was empty. She led me over to a square table with four seats, and we sat down. Still holding onto my hand, she looked at me again and said, "Oh my! This is unbelievable, Rosie *was* telling the truth all along.

"John," she continued, "before we go any further, let me tell you that you come from a very large family. I am the eldest of six girls. Your mother is the second one born, and there are four more after her. I have ten children living right here in central Florida. This evening you will get to meet most of them."

I was so taken aback by what was happening that I just sat there taking it all in. The entire time, Teresa never let go of my hand. She looked me in the eye most of the time while she spoke to me.

Finally I asked, "When will I get to see my mother?"

She had a plan. "Come to my house this evening, and we will call her on the phone. Just promise not to say anything to her while I speak. You can listen to her voice, but you have to promise not to say anything! Could you do that?"

I looked at her and said, "If that's what it takes to hear my mother's voice, I guess I can."

With that said, Teresa offered, "If you hang around for just a little longer, we can go from here directly to my house." Angie and I agreed to wait. I could hardly have done anything else. My emotions were so jangled that I just did not know how to respond to what was happening. All of my life I had waited for this moment, and now it was here. The years of anticipation, apprehension, anxiety, fear, and joy all came to the same intersection, and I had a difficult time sorting it all out. I did remember to call Val and tell her everything.

Angie and I went home with Teresa, but before the evening was up, my sister must have called me six times to remain updated on what was happening. I remember Val saying, "Whatever you do, wait until I get there before you meet Mom." She was on vacation in the Bahamas, and she said that she would come to Florida in a few days.

When the time came for the phone call to my mom, or Rosie, as Teresa kept referring to her, Teresa repeated, "John, you can listen on the other phone, but you must promise not to say anything!"

"I promise," I said. "But first tell me what your plan is."

She explained. "I'm going to try to convince Rosie to come to Orlando to visit me. And while she's here, I will take her to the final night of the talent search where she will see and hear you sing."

I thought, *I can see it now. My name is mentioned, I come out on the stage, she sees me, and then she has a heart attack.* I did not agree with the plan, but since I didn't have one of my own, I went along with it.

The house was full of people; most of them were my first cousins and their children. Teresa introduced me to her sons and daughters. They were all so kind to me. Some of them gave me a big hug and said, "Welcome to the family." Others said to me, "So you're Rosie's son. I've known your mother all my life. She's one of a kind."

"John!" Teresa called, "It's time to make the call. Take the phone in the kitchen. I'll be in the bedroom. Don't forget, don't say anything, just listen!"

With each ring of the phone, I felt as if I was in a movie, and I had no control over how the script was written. Everything was happening in a way that seemed so surreal.

"Hello, hello!" The voice on the other end of the phone said. "Who is it?"

Teresa responded, "Hi, Rosie. It's your sister Terry. What are you up to?"

"I'm taking care of Jimmy's kids, Peewee and Linda," Rosie answered. "What's up with you?"

"Well, I was thinking, how possible would it be to get you to come to Orlando to spend some time with me?"

"I would like to," Rosie answered, "but I can't do it right now. I've been watching the kids for Jimmy. Let's plan it for later on in the year."

Teresa pushed her appeal. "Rosie, I would like it if you came now. If money is the issue, I'll pay for your ticket to get here, that's no problem. I really would like to see you as soon as possible. What do you think?"

As I listened to her Island accent, it was all I could do not to yell into the phone. I soaked it all in to keep forever. *This is my mother's voice. I can't believe it! I just can't believe this is happening!* Honoring Teresa's request, I just listened to her and Rosie go back and forth, bartering for the upper hand. Rosie pretty much had her mind made up that she could not come to Orland any time soon.

Trying not to make her suspicious, Teresa gave in and said to her, "Well, I see that you have your hands full, so I'll let you go. I'll be in touch."

The conversation ended, and Teresa came out of her bedroom. She raised her hand and said, "John, it's not going to be as easy as I thought! I'm going to have to get one of our sisters to sit her down and tell her what's going on."

I asked my new aunt, "Why didn't you want me to say anything to her on the phone? Why did I have to be silent?"

Teresa sat me down on the couch in the living room and tried to explain. "John, for much of your mother's life, she said that she had children, but no one believed her. She would even purchase insurance policies with your and your sister's names as the beneficiaries. We thought that she was going off the deep end. Your mother and I are very close, and I believed her. But it became increasingly difficult to support this notion that she had children—other than your brother, Jimmy—because she could not tell us where you and your sister were. After a while, she just avoided talking about children. Sometimes, when the subject of children came up, she would walk away."

The next thing Teresa said startled me. "To deal with the pressure of justifying her other children, your mother made up a story that you both perished in a fire in New Jersey. She's been telling that story for eleven years. Not only is it her defense, to a great extent, she has come to believe it."

I looked at Teresa. All I could ask was "Why? What would make her tell a lie like that?"

Teresa tried to explain. "John, Rosie's had a difficult life. I don't think she's ever really gotten over leaving you and your sister. She tried to live a normal life, but I don't believe she could get away from her past. It has impacted everything about her. Now do you understand why it would have been so bad for you to speak to her on the phone? It could have led to a nervous breakdown or something like that."

I could understand that. "So, how are we going to handle this without hurting her any further? I do want to see her. I've waited all my life for this." Teresa decided that the best plan would be to have their sister Gloria break the news to Rosie.

The next day was Sabbath. I was surprised at how quickly the news had spread. It seemed as if everyone I talked to knew about it. I was scheduled to sing that morning in church. Just before I sang "The Lighthouse," I tried to explain what had happened. I couldn't get through the story, and I could not get through the song. I leaned forward on the pulpit and cried as I tried to sing.

When we arrived home from church, Aunt Sissy said, "John, your mother called. Call her right away, she's waiting!"

I dialed the number, and the phone rang only once before she picked it up. "John, is that you?" she asked.

"Mom!" Then there was a silence over the phone. I could hear her beginning to cry.

"John," she said, "I'm sorry, I'm sorry. Please forgive me. I only did what I thought was best for you. Please forgive me?"

I said to her, "Mom, I forgive you. I'm not concerned about the last twenty-five years. I'm just glad that God brought us back together." Even I didn't realize the impact that statement would have.

My mother tried to explain. "When you were born, your father and I were not married, and life was very hard for me in New York. You were very sick. Mrs. Haynes had such a special love for you—I knew that she and George could give you and Val everything that I could not. So I decided to leave you both there with them. The day I made that decision, I wrote a letter to the Lord and asked Him to return you to me one day. John, this is an answer to that prayer."

I could only say, "Mom, I understand. I forgive you. Mom, I want you to know that I love you. Forget about the last twenty-five years."

What she said next stunned me. "John, because you forgave me and said that you love me, I want to be what you are." What she meant is that she wanted to be a Christian, like I was.

"Mom, when will I get a chance to see you?" I asked.

"Soon, I hope," was her answer. That afternoon I called my sister and my aunt Teresa. We talked about making the arrangements for Rosie to come to Orlando.

The next thing I knew, the doorbell was ringing. I looked out the window and saw a news reporter with a camera crew standing at the door. "Hello," the reporter said. "Are you John Lomacang? We received a phone call about your story, and we would like to interview you, if that's all right."

"Sure, come on in," I said. It was all happening so fast. I had heard of miracles, but I had never been a part of one so public. That evening we were watching television, and every few minutes there would be a new flash, "Central Florida man finds his mother after twenty-five years, news at six!" Then later in the evening, the same thing again, "Central Florida man finds his mother after twenty-five years, news at eleven!" There I was for all of Florida to see. My time had finally arrived, my story was being told!

My sister arrived the next day. She cut her vacation short to make it there. Val asked, "Is it really true that you spoke to Mom? What did she say?" I told her everything about the conversation.

That evening I took her to meet her new aunt Teresa and her new cousins. When Teresa saw Val, she said, "Oh my, you look just like your mother." Val was warmly received, and there were questions galore. Teresa went through her picture collection to look for pictures of Mom. She found many. Our eyes were feasting on the pictures of a woman that Val scarcely remembered and that I didn't remember at all. We wanted to hear as many stories about Mom as we could and see as many pictures as Teresa found. We were not in a hurry for anything.

As I sat there, I realized the Lord had directed Maureen and me to sing "More Than Wonderful." He knew that in just a few short days, we would see how wonderful He really is. The saying is true: "God does work in mysterious ways."

In spite of the media's interest in our reunion, Teresa, Val, and I decided that it would be better if they were not at the airport when Mom arrived. It had been so many years, that we wanted the meeting to be private. When the day finally arrived, we woke up early to get to the airport on time. Angie, Val, and I were in one car with Teresa. Other cars were full of cousins. Everyone wanted to be there for Rosie's arrival.

She was arriving on Pan American Airlines via Miami. We waited at the gate, fidgety with anticipation.

The plane finally pulled in, the doors opened, and the passengers began to disembark. We lined the exit searching through the crowd for a glimpse of Rosie. People seemed to stream by forever, but suddenly there were no more passengers getting off the plane. We turned and looked at Teresa. She threw up her hands and said, "That's just like Rosie! She chickened out! She probably got off in Miami." The excitement died down as the wind was knocked out of our sails.

Just as we turned to walk away, one of the kids yelled, "There she is! There she is!" We hurried back to the exit ramp. I saw a little "Filipino-looking" lady, about five feet tall, walking as quickly as she could. She had a yellow canvas carry-on bag in one hand and a shoulder bag. I smiled from ear to ear as I took this all in. Angie was on one side and Val was on the other. We just stood and stared.

Rosie walked out of the exit and stopped right in front of me. She looked up at my six-foot two-and-a-half-inch frame and said, "How did you get so big?"

We grabbed each other and hugged as if there were no tomorrows. Val hugged her, and I hugged her. Mom was so small that she got lost between us. We all began to sob. The moment was so emotionally thick that tears were inevitable.

We sat down on one of the nearby benches and held onto each other for dear life. Mom closely examined my face and Val's. She gently outlined our faces with the palms of her hands. "My children are back," she whispered. We then held hands and walked off into the proverbial sunset as we exited the airport.

That evening we went to dinner with a ton of questions to ask. I wanted to make sure that this woman was really my mother. I began, "If you are really my mother, what did you leave me with when you left me with the Hayneses?"

In no time flat she had the answer. "That's easy! I left you with a blue-and-white hard shell small travel case. The interior was lined with red silk, and it had a little vanity mirror in the middle." She looked at me. "Am I correct?"

I was flabbergasted. "No one could have known that except my mother. I did not tell anyone about the suitcase. I vowed to keep it until I met you. When we get to the house, I'll show it to you." Then I pressed one other question forward. "OK, if you are really our mother, why do we call my sister Val when her name is really Vivian?"

Rosie answered quickly, "You couldn't figure that out all these years? If you take the first letter from each of her names, you get V.A.L. Her first name is Vivian, her middle name is Anita, and her last name is Lomacang. Put the first letter in each name together, and you get Val." Then she looked at both of us and said, "There are some things that only a mother knows."

That did it for me! Val and I looked at each other and concluded, "She's the real McCoy." The evening went on from one subject to another. One other thing we discovered that evening threw a wrench into the conversation.

I asked, "What about Jimmy? Is he really our brother?"

She replied, "Yes, he is. But he has a different father." Then she really startled us. "John, you and Val have different fathers also!"

Val and I looked at each other, both thinking, *What did she just say?*

She reiterated it. "Val, you and your brother John are my children, but you have different fathers." I saw the expression on my sister's face change. Just when we thought that our lives were complete, mother and father, Val found out that she was just getting the first piece to her puzzle.

"So, who is my father?" Val asked.

"He lives in St. Thomas," she answered. Then the conversation stopped, and we all just looked at each other. When we got home, I sat Rosie down and said to her, "Mom, I have a song I would like to sing to you. It's called "My Treasure." To me, you're like a treasure that I've been looking for all my life. Now that I've found you, I don't have to search anymore." As I sang, she sat there with her eyes filled with tears. I barely made it through the song myself.

That evening we had a long conversation about all of our pasts. Mom told about the decisions and circumstances surrounding her turbulent life. Val and I told ours. Time passed unnoticed. We talked until we just did not have any physical energy to go on.

Our visit was so short. We didn't have much time, because I had that prior commitment in California with the Heritage Singers. Val stayed in Orlando for a few days after I went to California. Then Mom went to New York to spend some time with Val and to greet Mr. Haynes, whom she had not seen in over twenty-five years. She waited to see me again before she went home.

When she finally returned to St. Thomas, it was to share the story of her newfound children, Vivian and John. We vowed to keep in touch by writing and calling each other as regularly as we could. Now I felt that my life was complete. Now I knew who I was and where I came from. Now I had a mother to call my own. No more mysteries. There were, of course, many questions I still needed to ask my mother, but now that I knew where she was, I could wait until we got to know each other better.

Me and my sister Vivian (Val) on the day we met my father (1971)

Second Grade - the year I found out my real last name was Lomacang.

Angie and I in New York before we were married.

The people who raised me – Momma Haynes (bottom left), Papa Haynes (right back), and Kelvin, my foster brother (right front) with relatives.

Mrs. Carmen Haynes, my "Momma"

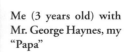

Me (3 years old) with Mr. George Haynes, my "Papa"

When I met my mother for the first time (July 1984).

The 1984 talent-search contest that got my name on the radio. John Lomacang and Maureen Mair-Tapp

My two years with the Heritage Singers—1984 (above) and 1985 (below)

My mother's baptism in 1989—one of the happiest days of my life. My mother, me, and Pastor Rheinhold Tilstra.

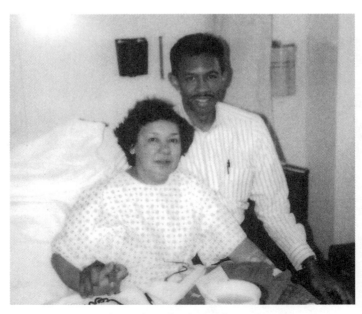

My mother and I in her hospital room in 1991.

My ordination service with Angie by my side and Elder Ricardo Graham speaking

My good friend Doug Batchelor who spoke for my ordination service.

Ed and Bonnie Ensminger celebrate with us.

Max and Lucy Mace join us on our special day.

My brother, Jimmy, my sister, Vivian.

Me and my good friend Cedric Walker

Teresa Lomacang, my aunt

Some of my family in St. Thomas

Johnny Parker

John Parker and Rosario "Rosie" Lomacang—my parents.

Rosario Maria Lomacang

Rosario Maria Lomacang—
modeling

My great-grandparents on my mothers side.

Teresa and Rosario in St. Thomas

Young Rosario at home on the Virgin Islands

Angela's siblings and her mother.

Vivian, Jimmy, Me, Angie, and my Aunt Eneida (1995).

John and Angie Lomacang today.

CHAPTER NINE

Look Out, World—Here We Come!

When my flight arrived in southern California, I was met by two of the Heritage Singers' musicians, Art Munar and Art Mapa. They helped me with my luggage and took me to the hotel where the group was staying during the recording sessions. That evening I met the rest of the singers. Coming from my background, their lifestyle was impressive. Their lives seemed so ideal—no problems, no bills, just traveling, singing, and seeing the world. It was like a fairytale, and I couldn't wait to join in.

Max Mace was so nice to me. "Hi, John," he boomed out. "Welcome to the Heritage Singers!" Then he introduced me to the others—the returning singers and the new members who were also just joining the group.

I finally got a chance to meet Val Mace. For years I had seen her perform, and I was honored to be in the same group with her. The other singers included Monty Jackson, Becky Trueblood (whom I found out had been selected Miss Idaho), Jackie Leiskie, Annie Mapa and Ted Atwood, the new bass singer. I was the new second tenor. Max sang baritone. I had already met his son Greg, who ran the sound. There was also a young guy from Poland named Merik Stekla.

I shared my story with Max about recently finding my mother, and he was amazed. "That will be a good story to share as we travel around the world," he said.

My three-day visit was up all too quickly, and I returned to Orlando. By then, Angie was almost fully packed and ready to make the move out West. However, there was one more piece of business to complete. I needed to put the engine of my car back together.

Robert and I got back to work on it. Surprisingly enough, in three days we were able to put it back together and get the engine started. After all of the parts were together, we had two screws left over. We joked that Toyota could have saved money on that engine by omitting those two screws.

I was amazed to hear so much doubt about the soundness of my engine. Family members told me that it couldn't be reliable enough to drive 3,000 miles. One said, "Call me when you break down, and we will send someone to get you." Angie's aunt was taking care of an older African–American lady from the south who stepped forward to encourage me when she heard that comment. "If the Lord could get Moses through the desert with one sandal on his foot, He can get you to California in any kind of car."

We prayed and bade everyone farewell. Aunt Sissy said, "Your room will be waiting for you when you come back." Angie's mom said, "I always wanted you to get a chance to see the world before you settled down. Now your chance has come. God be with you both."

Then it was time to go. We had three days to get from Orlando, Florida, to Placerville, California. We would have to average over one thousand miles a day to make it before our music workshop began on Sunday morning. The car was packed to the ceiling. We had everything we needed, except air conditioning for the car. If it wasn't hot enough in Florida that July, our trip would take us along the southernmost—the hottest—part of the United States.

I noted as we entered the state of Texas that we would have to travel 880 miles to reach the other side. We stopped near the middle of the state to prepare for the long drive through the desert. I purchased some coolant for the radiator and some spare fan belts in case the engine began to overheat. With nothing but road, rocks, cactus, and heat as far as we could see, we also stocked up on water and ice. Then I filled up the tank, and we headed for the open road.

About two hours later, Angie asked, "John, where are your car keys?"

"What are you talking about? They're in the ignition, of course!"

"No," Angie said, "they are not!" Sure enough, they were missing. My car was so old that you could start the car and slide the keys out without killing the engine. I had left the keys and the gas cap on the pump at the filling station. Fortunately, Angie had her keys, so we just stopped at the closest town and bought a new gas cap.

We saw wonderful sights along the way and occasionally stopped for scenic photos to preserve our memories of big cacti and high mountains. After nearly three full days of driving, we hit the southern California rush-hour traffic. This was our first time driving in California, and we had no idea how far we had to go. Angie was so tired by the time we reached California that she declared, "You can drive the rest of the way!"

"OK," I said. Since signs pointed to the left for Los Angeles and straight ahead for Sacramento, I figured that they must not be too far apart. "I'll drive until we get there."

About an hour later, I figured out that Sacramento was still nearly seven hours away and Placerville was beyond that. We stopped along the way to grab some fruit and take a few photos. "I can't wait to see these pictures," I said, as I took shot number 36. But the film didn't seem to be at its end. I took another shot of Angie, then she took one of me. When the camera showed that we were on shot number 40, I knew something was wrong. I slowly opened the camera, just in case, but as I peeked in, I saw what I had feared: There was no film in the camera! None!

Angie looked at me, and I looked at her. Then we laughed so hard we dropped our fruit. What else could we do? "Oh well," Angie finally said, "at least the memories are in our heads."

It was almost nine o'clock when we arrived in Sacramento. Thanks to Greg's final directions, we arrived at the Heritage Singers Ranch in

Placerville at exactly ten. To us, it looked like heaven. We saw lights inside, and when I rang the doorbell, someone called out, "Just push; it's open!"

We walked in to a whirlwind of friendly greetings as everyone made us feel at home. Finally Angie tapped me on the shoulder and whispered, "I'm tired. I want to go rest for a few minutes."

Lucy, Max's wife, showed us our room. "Welcome to your new home. I hope you like your king-size waterbed." She gave us some settling-in instructions and then invited us to the living room to "break the ice." We were the new kids on the block, and boy, did we feel that way.

That night when we went to bed, Angie said, "John, it's so dark here that it's hard to fall asleep." We were used to falling asleep in the midst of noise and light. Now we were in the foothills of the Sierras, and no lights shone through our window. All we could hear was insect sounds through our partially opened window. It was quite a stretch from Brooklyn, New York.

My very first concert with Heritage was at a large civic auditorium in Redding, California. I remember that Angie and Lucy stood in the back of the auditorium observing the new group, and after the concert, Lucy told Angie, "John looks like he wants to be the director. He moves his arms up and down as if he wants to direct the songs." We had a good laugh about that.

When I joined the group, I had many rough edges. But Max was patient with me. He has a special gift of dealing with different personalities, well-practiced through the years. Max has the ability to hear a voice with potential and take the time to shape it into something better than the singer had thought possible. I thought that I was a good singer when I joined the Heritage Singers, but what I became under experienced leadership was quite a bit more than I had foreseen.

In just a few months, our tour of Europe began. We flew to Belgium and then took the ferry across the English Channel to England, where we boarded our tour bus. It was customized with large windows and tables. One of the highlights of the tour was attending the Passion Play, held in Oberammergau, Germany once every ten years. The entire town is involved in casting the play that shares the life, betrayal, crucifixion, and resurrection of Jesus.

From there we went to Switzerland, Italy, Holland, Denmark, Austria, and several other countries. And this was just the beginning. In two short years, we traveled all over the world. We went to Brisbane, Caines, Hobart, Melbourne and Sydney Australia ; Papua New Guinea; Auckland, New Zealand; Tasmania; Tahiti; Singapore; Hong Kong; Paris, France; Innsbrook and Iskchel, Austria; Bacolod, Philippines; Holland; Milan and Mirano, Italy; Lugano, Switzerland; Brussels, Belgium; Jakarta, Indonesia; Bandung, Indonesia; Toronto, Canada; Vancouver, British Columbia, Honolulu, Hawaii, and more than forty other states in the United States.

Some days spent traveling on the bus left us so wrapped up in nonspiritual things that the concert that evening revealed our lack of spiritual strength. Other times, when we got on the bus and prayed and studied together, we had very spiritual concerts. Following these concerts, we would often say, "The difference was spending the day with the Lord."

Just living together on a forty-foot bus became a pain when we did not spend our time in prayer. Fifteen of us shared a space about twenty-five feet by five feet. That was home, every day. We sang every day except Mondays and Fridays. Sometimes we had two concerts on Sundays. We alternated between being a close family and a fragmented one. There were days when everyone wanted to quit and days when we wanted to sing together for the rest of our lives. In short, we were family. We experienced the greatest pain and the most delightful joys together.

All the while, the Lord was preparing me for greater things. My love for music drew me to the Heritage Singers ministry. During the first year, the 1984 to 1985 singing season, I found a desire to take the singing ministry to another level awakening in me. As we traveled, I saw the need for a deeper spiritual commitment to the Lord and not just to singing about and for the Lord.

While we traveled, I kept in touch with my mother. I sent letters, cards, pictures, and sometimes music. One of my greatest desires was to have her give her life to the Lord. I remembered she told me she wanted to be a Christian as I was. I gave her information on churches she could attend. I even sent Bible studies and literature for her to read. She would say to me, "I plan on going to church soon. I just need to make some time to go."

One of the strangest feelings I had while I was getting to know her took place when we were preparing for a concert. Mother's Day was coming, and the group members were buying cards and gifts for their parents. All of a sudden, while we were at the concert practicing, I blurted out, "Do you guys realize that this is the first Mother's-Day card I've bought in my entire life?" Things that others did routinely were a learning experience for me. The Lord was using me to slowly but surely fulfill the plan He had for my life and my mother's life. Angie was such a blessing during this time. She had such a good relationship with her mother that it allowed me to experience, through her life, what a healthy relationship with a mother should be.

It would take a whole book just to share our adventures in traveling. Our bus was burglarized in Paris. We experienced life-threatening turbulence on an airplane. Armed guards escorted us as we were invited to sing in Indonesia. We sang for ambassadors and prime ministers. We sang for the rich and the poor. We were in some of the most hair-raising car rides, some of the creepiest hotels, and some of the strangest churches.

In Australia, we fed kangaroos and took pictures with koalas. In New Zealand, we walked among a flock of sheep and had to watch where we stepped. We visited villages in New Guinea populated by dozens of children of the same father—the chief who didn't even know, himself, how old he was.

In Austria, Angie and I took a gondola ride to the top of the Austrian Alps, where we drank water from the snowmelt. In Indonesia, we received personally written formal invitations to the embassy, where we sang and dined with the ambassador of the United States. We sailed the English Channel and had lunch in the Eiffel Tower in Paris. While there, we also visited the ancient Notre Dame Cathedral. Artists lined the streets vying for an opportunity to paint our portraits.

The Lord was training me to work with people of varying backgrounds, belief systems, ideologies, likes, and dislikes. Growing up in Brooklyn, New York, I had dealt mostly with black people. In the Heritage Singers, I learned to deal with different cultures and different nationalities. The Lord really opened my eyes to allow me to see that no matter what your skin color, your heart and your mind were your greatest assets. Angie and I began to see people as humans first and not as categories.

Max would periodically ask me to make the altar call at the end of our concerts and invite people to give their hearts to the Lord. When I first tried, I was very nervous. I had the desire, but the skill was yet to be developed. Max would say to me, "John, just relax and think about what you are saying." The more I did it, the more comfortable I became. Ultimately, it was when I trusted the Lord to use me that my appeals had the most success.

On one of our albums, we were each given a nickname. Mine was "Pastor/Spiritual Leader." The furthest thing from my mind was being a pastor, but the Lord had different plans.

One evening when we were back in California, Max introduced the group to a hippy-looking guy named Doug Batchelor. He was not the kind of person I was accustomed to. Doug had a beard, and he was dressed in conflicting colors. Where I came from, in New York City, dressing well was very important. However, I discovered that Doug and I had more in common than I realized. First of all, he was also from New York. He had been in the world just as I was, before we met the Lord. His mother was in show business, and my father was a jazz musician. Doug did not have a close connection with his father, and neither did I. He was a prankster, and so was I. Yet, there was one more thing we discovered. Both of us liked reading and studying the Bible. We liked scriptural debates, and we rarely backed down from a discussion on any Bible topic. Before Doug left that evening, he said, "I sure would like to work with you one day." I seconded that notion.

Another important person in our Heritage Singer lives was Bonnie Ensminger. An avid historian and the right-hand person of Heritage

Singers, Bonnie was an anchor for Angie and me. She was the problem solver and source of sound advice that we often needed. Bonnie had worked for Heritage many years before we arrived. More than just booking the concerts, she and Lucy kept the group alive, while Max was gallivanting from place to place with the Singers.

I am convinced the Lord connected us with people who would have an impact on His plans for our lives. As we came to understand that, we learned to be careful how we treated everyone we met. We never know what role they will fulfill in our future.

In our second year with the Heritage Singers, Doug spent time with us on the bus. He didn't sing with the group, but he did the altar calls at the end of the concerts. As we got better acquainted, we joined forces as the pranksters of the group.

One day on a long bus trip to a concert, the girls decided to wear matching tennis shoes. Between our periodic stops for bathroom breaks and snacks, everyone fell asleep except for Doug and me. While they slept, Doug and I tied each person's shoestrings to someone else's. When we stopped again, we yelled, "Time to wake up! Bathroom break!" Then we stood at the front of the bus and watched everyone fall into a pile of bodies on the floor. Everyone went down except Doug and me. From that day on, they kept an eye on us, especially when we were in the back of the bus laughing. Doug didn't spend the entire year with us. After about a month, he returned to his work as an evangelist. He vowed that he was going to try to get me to work with him in evangelism.

Our last year with the Heritage Singers was the fifteenth year of the ministry. A large reunion concert was planned at the convention center in Anaheim, California. The highlight to me was not the music but the opportunity to have my mother, Rosie, my aunt Teresa, and my mother-in-law, Mrs. Marr, spend the last week of our tour with us. They traveled with us to the concerts and were special guests at the Heritage Reunion Concert. It was a bittersweet experience, the ending of one phase of our lives and the beginning of another. Our two-year commitment was up, and it was time to go back home to Orlando. Angie was extremely happy. She wanted to be wherever her mother was. I wanted to be wherever Angie was.

The day of the reunion concert was a sad day. We spent the day saying our last goodbyes to our Heritage Family. The pains and the joys we had shared made us all that much stronger to face the world that now lay before us. Max and Lucy had been so gracious to us. "Whenever you are a Heritage Singer, you are one for life," Max said.

Lucy gave us a hug and said in her traditional way, "Take care, kids. Keep your mother posted. We'd love to have you keep in touch."

We had made so many friends, and we knew that wherever they ended up and wherever we ended up, we would always share a bond that neither time nor circumstance could sever.

Angie and I looked back on the lives the Lord had allowed us to impact through our work with the Heritage Singers. We had developed a love for touching people's hearts and leading them to Him. The Heritage Singers ministry was such a blessing to us. We would not trade those two years for anything but being with Jesus in heaven.

The sun was setting on our two-year whirlwind journey, and it was time to go. We knew we had a long road ahead of us, both literally and symbolically. We did not know what we wanted to do, but we did know that our view of life was now vastly different from before.

Angie and I vowed not to rush home, as we had rushed to California. We wanted to take our time going back to Florida—five days, at least. We were going to stop and take in the sights, and this time we were going to make sure we had film in our camera.

The journey was filled with joy, because we knew we had family waiting for us at the other end. Angie cried out, "We're going home! We're going home!" I enjoyed our time in California, but I, too, could not wait to get home.

We drove and we drove and we drove. After two years, our car still did not have a properly working air conditioner. The compressor cooled the air, but the fan didn't work. The only way to get cool air into the car was to drive fast and allow the outside air to blow through the vents. Believe me, in that hot weather, I drove fast!

We had a few incidents. One night as we drove through the desert, our taillights stopped working. I had to drive for miles without taillights until I found a gas station. When I pulled off the road, I knew the majority of the journey was still ahead of us and that we were in no position to pay for costly repairs. So, I did what I thought was best. Angie and I prayed that the problem would be remedied. Then I lifted the hood and looked in the engine compartment. You know how it is—I was hoping to find that big "on and off switch" that is supposed to fix the problem. Nothing looked visibly loose. I just shook the wires that I saw, and suddenly Angie yelled, "The lights are back on!" It was a direct answer to our prayers.

We were still over two thousand miles away from home but on pace to cover it in the same three days as before. After we got through Texas, the longest state in the journey, there was an adrenalin rush, and we just made up our minds to get home. By the time we passed through the tip of Alabama, Angie was exhausted, and I had to do the driving.

But when I announced, "Angie, we're in Florida!" she forgot how tired she had been. Four hours later, we arrived home to a hero's welcome, glad to be back where we belonged. But when the welcome-home celebration died down, a question still burned in our minds.

"Where do we go from here?"

CHAPTER TEN

The Power of Faith

Monday morning came soon enough, and we knew we had to get back into the "real world." Angie and I found that our biggest hurdle with potential employers was convincing them that we had been employed in a marketable profession for the past two years. Many seemed to think that traveling with a singing group had not prepared us for the job market. The Lord knew that our experiences had prepared us for the future. But we had to find that out for ourselves.

I wanted to work full time, but I didn't realize how unready I really was. After traveling for two years, being in a different location almost every day, it was difficult to stay in one place too long. I got a job doing clerical work at a bank, but after two days I quit. I told Angie that I just felt trapped, that it was impossible to sit at the same desk day after day. We turned to part-time jobs to get back in rhythm with the working world.

Between unemployment and part-time jobs, we survived day-to-day for three months. Then I finally got a job that I stuck with. I was hired as a junior accountant for an excavation construction company. Despite the fact that the owner was a Christian, he had no problem using profanity when things did not go his way. However, the Lord blessed, and after a month, Angie was hired there also. We drove to work together and enjoyed spending the entire day together. It seemed natural after the past two years.

We were able to move out of Angie's aunt's house into our own apartment. But we couldn't get any credit (the past two years with the Heritage Singers weren't considered legitimate employment), so we couldn't afford to furnish our place. So we did the next best thing; we bought a used bed and table and one white plastic recliner. We readjusted to regular life, but it didn't feel right. We began to see that the Lord had other plans for us.

Before we left California, Doug Batchelor tried to get us to stay and work with him in evangelism. At that time, it didn't seem workable, and besides, we wanted to go home. However, Doug called me from time to time to fly out and work with him in short meetings. The second time, I worked with him in a crusade held at the Sacramento Carmichael SDA Church. The pastor introduced me to the congregation and said, "Instead of having John fly back and forth to work with Pastor Doug, let's write the conference and ask them to hire him." The congregation responded with a hearty Amen.

I was honored by the gesture. Before I returned home, I went with Doug to a meeting of pastors, where I met Elder Richard Simons, the president of the Northern California Conference. He said, "So you're John Lomacang. Every time Doug has meetings, he wants to work with you."

As much as I loved the work, I was not in any position to ask the conference to hire me. All that I had done to that point was sing and preach whenever I was given the opportunity. I did know my Bible very well, and I enjoyed giving Bible studies and leading people to Christ.

After the crusade was over, I returned home to my boring job. My local church recognized the moving of the Lord in my life and asked me to be a deacon. The pastor included me in more of the outreach of the church. But every day, I was faced with the reality that unless a miracle happened, I was stuck in a dead-end job. One day Angie walked past my office and asked, "John, what's wrong?"

The answer burst out of me. "There has to be more to life than this. I want to be in the ministry!"

THE POWER OF FAITH

She said exactly the right thing. "Let's pray about it." And we did.

I kept searching for a place where the Lord would be able to use me in pastoral ministry. But the fact of the matter was that I had no formal training or education that would qualify me for pastoral ministry. If the door were going to open, it would have to be by the Lord's hand. I had nothing but the desire. Still, we really wanted to stay close to family for a while. We kept praying, "Lord, please open the door to ministry for us. We will be willing to go anywhere, except California."

Problems began sprouting up everywhere. My ten-year-old Toyota Corona was falling apart. The company owner's daughter was a faith-talking Christian. She said, "Honey, you need to get rid of that car and get you what you want!" Then she offered to have the company loan us the money for a down payment.

Angie and I went to a Toyota dealership and picked out a Toyota 4-Runner. We wrote a check for the $3,500 down payment and applied for the loan—even though we didn't qualify for a much smaller furniture loan. We prayed, "Lord, if it is your will that we get this car, please let us know by allowing the loan to go through."

About 10:30 the next morning, we got a call from Toyota. The salesperson said, "Your loan has been approved, and we are going to deposit the check in the bank!"

I smiled from ear to ear. Angie and I stopped to thank the Lord. We knew it was His plan for us to have this vehicle, because we had asked it to happen only if it was His will.

I went to Arlene's office to get the check for the $3,500 advance. She frowned as she said, "I know I told you that we would, but my father says that the company can't loan you that money. I'm sorry."

When Angie heard, she shed a tear and asked, "What do we do now?"

I reminded her of our prayer. "The loan went through. Do you think the Lord answered our prayer?" We prayed again, but I thought to myself, *If Toyota wants to open a dealership on the moon, now would be a good time, because our check is going to bounce that high!* Immediately I rejected that thought. I knew that everything that had happened in our lives was the result of one miracle after another. I knew nothing was impossible for the Lord. Once I heard someone say, "Never expect a thousand-dollar answer to a ten-cent prayer!" We needed a $3,500 answer, and our prayer allowed our faith to take hold of God's ability.

I told Angie, "Give me some time. I know that the Lord will impress me what to do!" Less than an hour later, I told her "The Lord laid it upon my heart that I should make two phone calls."

When I told her whom I would be calling, she wasn't so sure. "One of those people you hardly know, and the other one, you know so well that you ought to know that he will say No!"

I was somewhat skeptical, but I did not ever utter one word of doubt. I made the two phone calls, and before twenty minutes were up, both parties said Yes! The money was being wired to our bank that day, that hour.

When I told Angie, she said, "That's amazing!"

"That's the kind of God we serve," I said. "What else should we expect?" When the day was over, the vehicle was ours, and the check was covered. Praise the Lord! We saw the obvious blessings, and we had much for which to thank the Lord. But what He was about to do was far greater than we could have ever imagined.

Things at work became more difficult as the owner became angrier and more difficult. As we searched for other employment, we realized how fortunate we were not to owe the company all that money. The Lord knew exactly what He was doing. The more we trusted Him, the easier it became to follow Him.

Our prayers became more pointed. We continued to ask the Lord to open the doors for us in ministry. One evening while we were praying, we realized we were placing limits on the Lord. We were praying to go anywhere, except California. We changed our prayer to "Lord, we will go anywhere, including California."

That Sunday afternoon, we ran into some friends at the mall. "You guys are so hard to reach," they said. "You're never home!" Angie and I decided that we needed an answering machine, so we purchased one that was on sale.

At work the next day, Angie said, "I can't wait to get home to see if we have any messages." Angie was fond of the phone. No matter where she was, she called her family as often as possible. As soon as we arrived home that evening, Angie darted into the bedroom and called out, "The light is blinking. We have messages!"

"Wait for me," I asked. "I want to listen to the messages with you." When we heard the first message, we could only stare at each other in disbelief. The very first message on our answering machine was from the president of the Northern California Conference.

He said, "I would like to have you return my call. There is something brewing out here in California, and I want to talk to you about it. If I'm not available when you call, ask for Elder Larry Caviness. We look forward to hearing from you soon."

I had to sit down. "California! Angie, we have been praying for one solid week that we will be willing to go anywhere—including California! Just one week later, the prayer is answered!" It was already too late to return the call, but I could hardly wait for morning. The Lord was not only developing our faith, He was working on our patience also.

That night, our prayers took the form of praise. We knew the Lord was working out something we could not yet comprehend, and we wanted to thank Him in advance for it. Following our prayers, Angie and I just lay there thinking and talking with the light off until we fell asleep.

When we picked up the phone the next morning, we weren't sure "what was brewing," so we assumed nothing. After getting through to Elder Caviness, we listened as he unfolded our future. He said, "A few months ago, we received a letter, and in it was a check for $12,000 made out to us to be given to you. The person who wrote the letter was requesting that we give you an opportunity in ministry in this conference for one year. They requested to have you work with Pastor Doug Batchelor in evangelism. The commitment would be for only one year."

Angie and I stared at each other. Elder Caviness asked, "What do you think about that?"

I was so elated that all I could say was, "Great!"

Elder Caviness made it clear. The conference was not hiring me. There would be no benefits, no coverage of any kind. After one year, there was no promise of employment. He ended the conversation by saying, "We want you to pray about it."

We sat stunned. Once again, the Lord went far beyond our highest expectations. We dropped to our knees and thanked Him. Then we talked to Angie's mother, who encouraged us and wished us well. Before the next day was over, we called and said, "Yes!" Elder Caviness also informed us that the Vallejo church would be willing to pay me an additional small stipend to serve as their youth pastor when I was not on the road with Doug. That would certainly help us make ends meet.

Doug called soon and asked if we could be there shortly for a series he would be holding. We gave one week's notice at our jobs and prepared to move. We did not know what the future held beyond that commitment, but we were sure the Lord was the One holding the future.

It soon become clear why we were able to get a car loan and not a furniture loan. We needed the truck to move, and if we had been able to fill our apartment with furniture, we would have had to leave it all behind, as we did the white plastic recliner.

We said our goodbyes with tears of joy and headed down the road to California once again. Two days into our journey, it finally hit us that this was not a vacation—it was the beginning of a new life. Angie broke down and cried. I held her as we began to adjust to the idea that we would be living away from our families permanently.

When we arrived in Vallejo, Pastor William Hull gave us directions to a reasonable hotel until we found an apartment. Then he and his wife, Carole, invited us to their home for dinner. Their kind friendliness made us feel welcome.

We quickly learned that the little money we had wouldn't go far. Each apartment complex we looked into wanted a security deposit, plus the first and last months' rent. Some places wanted to see a local work history or didn't rent to people moving into the state. By the end of the second day, we were very discouraged, and our money supply was shrinking fast. Angie said, "We still have enough money to get home if we leave tomorrow." I was beginning to think the same things.

Just as we began to self-destruct, the Lord redirected our attention. I picked up the newspaper and saw something that I had missed all day—a one-inch square advertisement that said in bold letters, "**$75 Dep.**" After two days we were desperate, ready to take anything. I dialed the number and asked, "Are any apartments left for rent?"

She said, "Yes, just one."

The office would be closing in fifteen minutes. "Let's go," I called to Angie. We jumped in the truck and followed the directions to a beautiful complex with a fountain, a pool, and a nice clubhouse. We filled out the application and left with the manager's promise to call us as soon as a decision was made tomorrow. The next day could not come fast enough.

When she hadn't called by 10:00 a.m., I called her. "This is John Lomacang. My wife and I were there last night. Have you heard anything yet?"

"Hold on," she said. About a minute later she reported, "I'm looking at your paper work. You have been . . . approved."

Then I asked the all-important question. "How much will it take to move in?"

She put me on hold. After two minutes, she had an answer. "Sir, we are running a special. The deposit is only $75. We will also prorate the rent, which means that it will cost only $238 to get in."

"We will be right there!" I shouted. We grabbed our clothes, checked out, hooked up the trailer, and headed over there. Not only did we get the model apartment—the one with all the bells and whistles, but the lights and the phone were already connected. And the number on that apartment door confirmed to us that God was completely in charge—it was apartment number 7!

I was taken aback again with how meticulous the Lord is. He had thought of all the details and left nothing undone. We just had to stop and thank Him.

CHAPTER ELEVEN

Starting Over

We settled in very well. Pastor Hull introduced us to the church on Sabbath. The ethnically diverse congregation accepted us warmly. The youth group got off to a good start and grew each week. Church work was foreign to us, but Pastor Hull walked me through it. I learned a great deal from him.

I really enjoyed being on the road in evangelism with Doug. Singing, teaching, and leading people to a relationship with the Lord really made my pulse quicken. Doug and I worked well together and developed a real friendship. He was easy to work with, and together we had a great deal of fun—we knew when to be serious and when to goof off. But these trips kept me away from my wife for days at a time.

The eleven months that Doug and I worked together was a time of growth for me. Evangelism was so much more rewarding than even I thought it would be. We saw lives changed, homes in conflict made whole, and sad and suffering people find the joy of following Jesus. Our youth ministry in the Vallejo church was going strong, and we were not looking forward to it's ending. We had really become attached to the young people. We had seen their lives change, and we knew they had changed us, as well.

I tried repeatedly to find out who had donated the money that allowed us to do this wonderful work. But the conference officers refused to say. Then I was asked to sing at the funeral of a woman who was very fond of me. At the funeral, it was said that she helped many people with anonymous financial gifts. It seemed clear to me that the reason I had been invited to sing was because I was one of those people whom she helped "anonymously." From then on, I shared the impact of her generosity as I told how God had blessed my life.

With just one month remaining in our agreed time at Vallejo, we had no idea about the future. The conference had not offered us any further employment. Pastor Hull had given us no indication of any change in plans.

Doug asked, "What are you planning to do after next month?"

"I have no idea," I answered.

He had already tried to get the conference to continue our program for another year. "They said No," he reported. I told Doug that Angie and I were praying for an opportunity to work in ministry together, because I didn't want to continue traveling without her. What he said next surprised me. "John, if you think that you are going to be hired and given your own church to pastor after being in this conference for less than one year, think again. They don't do things that way."

I think Doug momentarily forgot about the miracles in his own life. Things often worked out in unusual ways for him also. I felt that if the Lord could do it for Doug, then He could do it for me also. That evening, Angie and I asked the Lord to give us direction. We needed to have our faith strengthened, because we did not know what to do after the conference's commitment ended.

Things started to happen. Elder Dwayne Corwin, the conference ministerial director, asked me to meet with him in his office. "John," he asked, "what would be your ideal church to pastor? Would it be Caucasian, African-American, or mixed?"

I had an answer. "My ideal congregation would be mixed. But it really doesn't matter, because to me, people are people, not categories."

A week later, the conference president talked to me about the work in northern California and asked what I saw as God's plan for me. It was an encouraging development, but our meeting ended quickly. The very next day, Elder Hal Thompson asked me to join him at a pastors' meeting. He said, "John, we have been watching you for the last eleven months, and we would like to extend a task-force opportunity to you and your wife. There's a church we'd like to have you pastor for the next two years. What do you think?"

What I thought was, "If I want to stay in the ministry, what options do I have?" But I listened as he told me more about the church. "The church is in a town called Weaverville. It's a beautiful little church, and the congregation of mostly older people are very friendly."

Once again I heard the Lord talking to me. I could almost hear Him say, "Trust Me. I've never led you wrong, and I never will."

Elder Thompson said to me, "What do you think? Would you like to see it?"

"Sure I would," I answered.

"Go up and see the church," he said. "Preach a sermon there. Meet the people. We have a parsonage there, and you won't have to pay rent." He left the punch line for last. "However, instead of paying you $1,500 a month, your stipend will be $500 a month. Discuss it with your wife and get back to me soon."

I could not wait to tell Angie the news. When I was sharing it with her, both of us began to cry, because we knew the Lord was removing the walls one brick at a time.

The very next Sabbath we drove to Weaverville. The beautiful church was located up in a small mountain community—and it was so empty that morning you could have fired a shotgun without endangering anyone. The church service was quite different from anything I had experienced. I was raised in a 1,200-member church that was packed each Sabbath. I guess the Lord really wanted to teach me something completely new.

But after church, the fellowship was so sweet. Even though we were not the same complexion as the rest of the church members or people in town, we were warmly received. The parsonage—located about thirty steps from the rear of the church—was quaint and clean. We concluded that if this was what the Lord wanted for us, then this was what we would accept.

After tearful, heartfelt goodbyes at Vallejo, we left for the high country. With my $1,000 a month cut in pay plus the loss of Angie's job—and the poor prospects of her finding another one in such a small town—we faced some interesting times and tests of faith. Many of the members helped us get the furniture and boxes into the parsonage. One of the first questions we heard was, "Do you have a four-wheel drive vehicle? You're going to need it here!"

I looked at Angie, and she nodded as if she was reading my mind. When we were in Orlando, we did not know why we bought a 4-by-4. But now we knew. The Lord was way ahead of us. He knew we would be in Weaverville long before we knew that we were even going to be in California.

We had a lot to learn about living in the country. The church members taught me about wood-burning stove inserts. I learned how to use an ax and that "kindling" was not another word for family or kinfolk. The Lord worked miracle after miracle for us in that small town.

One Sabbath morning, we had only eighty dollars left until payday, which was a week away. Angie had not yet found employment. My tithe was seventy-five dollars, and my car insurance was also seventy-five dollars. I made up my mind I needed to give faithfully if I wanted the members to give faithfully also. When I returned my tithe, we prayed for the Lord to step in and close up the gap. That evening, Angie and I went to the post office to get our mail. In it was a letter from someone we had never met, along with a check for $238. In the lower left corner of the check, they had written: "Because you preach the gospel." The Lord moved on the heart of someone far away to supply our need.

I was still able to join Doug for an evangelistic series occasionally. Not long after our move, he invited us up to his house after a series. That Sunday afternoon, the sun was hot enough to enjoy a cool float on tubes in his pond. In the middle of our conversation, Doug said, "John, I wish you would stop lying!"

I was stunned. "Doug, what am I lying about?"

"For almost the whole year that we worked together, you told people that a woman who had died donated the twelve thousand dollars that gave you a chance in ministry. How did you come up with that idea?"

I explained what I had heard at the funeral. "When I asked if that lady was the one, I was told, 'She could have been!' That's why I concluded that she was."

Doug looked at me, "If you only knew how much it bothered me to hear you share that story."

I was totally confused. "Doug, why did that upset you? Do you know different? Do you know who donated the twelve thousand dollars?"

Doug smiled. "Yes, I know."

Angie and I looked at each other. We had been trying for so long to find out! "Doug, would you please tell us?" I asked. "We're supposed to be friends! I promise not to let the person know that I found out."

Doug was turning red. He interrupted me, "If you would stop talking, I'd tell you who it was." I shut up. He said, "John, it was me. I gave the money for you to work in evangelism with me."

Angie and I just floated there, astonished. We were at a loss for words. Finally, I leaned up on the tube and said, "Why didn't you tell me?"

"I wanted to work with you without your feeling that you owed me," he said. "If I told you, our year of working together might have been tense. You would have felt so obligated to me that it would probably have messed up our friendship. I wanted our working relationship to be based on friendship, not finances."

What could I say? "Doug, thank you from the bottom of my heart. Because of your gift, I am now the pastor in Weaverville. If you had not been willing to let the Lord bless me through you, I would most likely still be in Florida. Tell me—why did you do it?"

He said, "We worked so well together when you flew out to help me in evangelism. We have so much in common—we're both from

New York, we both enjoy evangelism—we could be ourselves with each other. I knew that working with you would be easy, and I was right. I was hoping the conference would keep us together because, after less than a year, we were the most requested team in the conference."

"We can still work together," I assured him. "It won't be as often now, but just give me a call, and I'll be glad to help when I can. It's the least I can do."

"Oh, don't worry," he said with a smile, "I'll be calling you. I'm not going to let you get away that easy! If I have anything to say about it, we'll work together again often!"

I look back and realize that each intersection of life had a purpose. Being in the Heritage Singers meant more than singing. It was the place where the Lord developed in me the gifts that were necessary to serve Him. It was the place where the Lord introduced me to the men He would use to open the door. The Lord chose Max Mace to get me to California, and He chose Doug to keep me here. Thanks, Max! Thanks, Doug! Thank You, Lord, for true friends!

Before much time had gone by in Weaverville, my niece came to live with us. Tiashia was fresh out of New York City. Northern California was a very different place for her, but she needed to get out of the city, and we were giving her a new start. My sister, Vivian, was getting her life on a new track, and having Tiashia with us gave her the time and space she needed. It was a challenge to have another person to care for—especially in our very small house—but it was nice to have someone with whom we could share our love.

Then we got another surprise—a phone call from my mother. She said, "I have so much to tell you. I followed your advice and asked a pastor to pray with me about my addiction to alcohol and cigarettes. He prayed with me, John, and I have not touched either one since. I've been clean for months, and I don't even have the desire for them anymore."

I was filled with joy. "I'm so glad you decided to trust your life to the Lord." She also told me she was enjoying food again and had gained some healthy weight. Then she dropped the bombshell. "By the way,

John, I am on my way to California to live with you. Remember, you told me I was welcome."

I had told her that several years before, but she hadn't mentioned it since. I could hardly think enough to ask, "Are you in St. Thomas now? When do you plan to come to California?"

"I already left St. Thomas," she said. "I'm in Miami. I leave soon on an Amtrak train that should get me to you in about a week."

I whispered to Angie, "My mom is on her way to live with us. She should be here in a week!" Angie placed her hand under her throat and opened her mouth in shock. What could I say? "Just call when you get your arrival information, and we'll pick you up."

Our house was about to get much smaller. Angie and I were happy but apprehensive. I had only seen my mother on two short occasions in my life, and now she was coming to live under our roof. Everything seemed to be happening at once—a new pastorate, new church, new church family, new family, and new mother. I had to mentally prepare myself to call Rosie "Mom"—something almost entirely new for me.

The day she arrived at the station, I jumped out of the car to give my mom a big hug. It was almost like the day when we met for the first time. But she looked so different! A bright smile lighted up a face much more free of stress and burdens. "Are you glad to see me?" she asked.

"Mom, of course I'm glad to see you!" At dinner I had to ask, "Mom, what made you leave everything in St. Thomas to move to California?"

"John" she replied, "I just got sick and tired of the same old life. After I quit smoking and drinking, I needed to get away from those places and people. I couldn't think of a better place to be than on the other side of the world with my son."

She sounded as good as she looked. "Mom, you are going to love living in Weaverville. It's so quiet you'll be able to clear your mind from the past."

I have to admit that I was hoping for a real "mother and son" talk that would clear up the thousands of questions I still had about her life.

Even though I had forgiven her, I needed to know more about the decisions she had made. I could only hope she would be willing to talk.

That evening before we went to bed, we prayed that the Lord would accomplish His purpose for all of us. For years, I had been praying that my mother would accept the Lord in her life. I could only pray that as her pastor and her son, I would not do anything to hinder the Lord from leading her.

The church welcomed Mom warmly, and she handled their questions easily. I began to see that in many ways, I was like my mother—outgoing, confident, and never at a loss for words. Angie said, "John, I can't believe how much alike you are, since you never lived together."

As time passed and we became more comfortable with each other, Mom agreed to talk about her past. I asked, "Mom, when you left us, why didn't you come back for us, even after a few years?"

"I did come back for you," she said, "but there was a 'for sale' sign on the house where I left you, and I thought the people had taken you and Val."

"What did you do then? Did you report it to the authorities? Did you continue to search?"

She said, "I was so distraught I gave up!"

That made me a little angry. "How could you give up on Val and me? We waited for years for you to return!"

She was getting visibly uneasy. "What did you want me to do? I told you the house was sold! Where did you expect me to look?"

"Mom," I said, "I am having a difficult time believing you, because the house where we lived is still there to this day. It was never sold. Mr. and Mrs. Haynes inherited that home from their family, and they never moved."

Then she changed her story. "John, maybe I was a little intoxicated when I came back to look for you! I can't remember."

I calmly pressed my questions. "Mom, even if you were intoxicated, why didn't you try again after you were sober?"

Then she said something that I knew was not true. She said, "Maybe I forgot where the house was. Maybe the cab driver took me to the wrong house, since it was raining that night." When she saw that I was not buying that line, tears came to her eyes. "John, your father and I were not able to get along. We weren't married, and I was young and far away from home. I didn't know what to do, so I panicked! I knew that the Haynes could provide you with the things I could not. They had a house, and they loved both of you. Mrs. Haynes would not even let me take you out in the night air when you were an infant. She even told me on several occasions that you were 'her son.' With that kind of love, I knew I could not go wrong leaving you there."

As she saw that I was still struggling with feelings of abandonment, she said, "John, when I left you, I didn't know if you were going to live or die. You were sick when you were born, and I didn't how how to take care of you. Mrs. Haynes was the mother that I knew I could not be. She was nursing you back to health. I felt sure I was doing the right thing."

Finally she said, "John, look at how your life turned out. Aren't you glad I didn't raise you? I know that if I had, you would not be where you are today."

I could only nod. "I guess you're right. I am pleased with how my life turned out." I decided to give Mom room to get her life off to a new start. She enrolled in a nursing program that was being offered at the Weaverville hospital. But times were tense in our home. She wanted immediate "motherly respect," and I just couldn't generate that so quickly. After one angry confrontation, I realized that the devil was trying to get me to push my mother away, and I was not going to let him get the upper hand. I apologized to her, and she was so taken off guard by it that she muttered under her breath, "Yeah, me too!"

After that, we got Mom an apartment. It was hard for her at first, but we had to do something if our growing relationship was to have any chance at all. And she did well. She got her driver's license and saved up enough money to buy a car.

I knew that my mom was proud of me. When I went to her apartment, she had my picture on her dresser. She would say, "I play the Heritage Singers album all the time. I love listening to your voice. Whenever I miss you, I play your song."

Our relationship was making headway. I wanted to know more about our family, about the brother I had never met. But she made it clear that she wasn't ready to talk about her past. Someday, she promised, but she needed time.

That next week was my birthday. I was sure Mom would come to church to celebrate with us, but she didn't show up. After church, I went to see her. "Your birthday brings up too many sad memories," she said. "Those were hard times. As a matter of fact, when I was pregnant with you, I thought I had a cyst. Exploratory surgery showed that I was pregnant."

They didn't have home-pregnancy tests in those days. She went on. "Then I had to figure out what to do with you. I was afraid that if I took you and your sister back to the Virgin Islands, my parents would take you away from me, like they had with your brother."

I ventured a question. "Mom, how long were you in New York before you went back to the Virgin Islands?"

"I was in New York until 1964, the year your grandmother was killed."

She was in New York for eight years of our lives, and we did not hear from her at all. "Mom, didn't you think about Val and me while you lived in New York? How did you feel on our birthdays?"

She admitted that it was tough but refused to say more. She told me about her long relationship with a white man named Jim Miller and about how the racial tension in those days would have made it hard for them to raise us. "I knew that you and Val were well taken care of and that coming back into your lives would only complicate things—especially since I did not have anything or any place of my own to keep you."

Remembering our stable lives with the Hayneses, I couldn't disagree with her. But she was placing the blame on everyone but herself. So I pressed the question, "Mom, I think that you just didn't want us. You were enjoying your life without the responsibility of having to raise your children."

She became very defensive. "How could you say that I did not want you? I told you that the circumstances were not right. What more do you want me to say?"

After we shared some birthday cake, she said, "John, I am so proud of you, and I want you to know I really do love you. One of the reasons why I chose to come here was to get to know you better. There are things about my past I am not proud of and some things I cannot change. I promise that if you give me some time, I will try to make it up to you. We missed a lot of years, and I know it was mostly by my choice, but we could take it from here and move on."

I could see the sincerity and the sorrow in her eyes. There were things we both knew could never be reconciled. But I hugged her and thanked her for being open with me. I had to keep in perspective that the Lord had other plans for us. I believed He moved on her heart to come to Weaverville. I had to make sure I did not become a stumbling block to His plans.

About this time, I was planning my first solo evangelistic series. I worked hard to prepare the slides and the sermons. I blitzed Weaverville with information about the Revelation Seminar and decided to rent the town hall to make room for all I hoped would attend. My mission was twofold. On the one hand, I wanted the town to know about the truths of the Bible. On the other, I wanted to do my best, so my mother would understand the message well. She had not yet been baptized, and I knew that these meetings very well could be the method the Lord would use to reach her.

On opening night, the hall was packed. There was a great deal of interest but also much opposition from the other churches in town. Several started competing seminars, and some pastors worked hard to convince their members not to attend. I met their opposition straight on and kept pointing people to Bible truth. Attendance decreased significantly when we moved the meeting to the church, but I preached five nights a week for five weeks and baptized several people.

Even more than the teachings of the church, my mother was most impressed about baptism. She said, "I am so glad I can get a new start at life, and I can have my past forgiven. You don't understand how freeing that is. I feel as if the whole world has been taken off my shoulders. John, could you baptize me?"

By far, the highest point of the series was when I had the opportunity to baptize her. My mother hadn't missed a single meeting. She did her homework, read the Bible, and came each night anxious to learn. She said, "John, when I was being raised, I did not know that the Bible even taught these things. I am so glad to see that the Bible can be trusted."

I grabbed my mother and swept her off her feet in a hug. "Of course I will baptize you. There is nothing in the world that would bring me greater joy than to be able to present you to the Lord!"

Because I was not a licensed minister, I asked another pastor to lead out in the service. But there was not a dry eye among the people when I stood with my mother in the Trinity River and said; "I now baptize you in the name of the Father and the Son and the Holy Spirit." She was the first person I ever baptized.

As I looked into her eyes, I knew then that the Lord had been working out this moment all of our lives. I realized why He had not allowed me to meet her years before, when I was younger and my anger would have pushed her away. The Lord was waiting until the right time before removing the obstacles that kept me from finding her. It took over thirty years to get to the place where my mother and I were finally on the same page. We not only shared a similar bloodline, but we were both now saved by the Blood of the Lamb Christ Jesus.

I felt like Moses. His mother gave him up at three months old to save his life, and he was the youngest of his siblings. He had an older brother and an older sister, and the Lord was developing in him the gifts needed to lead others out of a life of bondage to sin—so many similarities to my own life. The Lord was preparing me for something beyond my wildest dreams—the opportunity to lead others to Christ.

CHAPTER TWELVE

My Biological Mother

"John, there is an opening in the Antioch church, and we would like to have you interview for that position."

The voice on the phone was the conference president. And his words were like a dream come true. Our agreement with the conference was for two years of service at Weaverville, on a stipend. After about twenty-two months, we had begun to wonder if we would be able to continue in ministry. The president continued. "This is not another stipend-basis assignment. This would be a full call to be a licensed minister, with all the salary, benefits, and rights as any of our licensed ministers."

The Lord was opening doors that less than two years before were only a blur in my dreams. Angie's mother was visiting, and Angie was home for lunch, so when I hung up the phone, I shouted the news. "Can you imagine? The Lord has done it again!" We prayed and thanked Him for making a way for us. Less than three years before, we had prayed to be in the ministry, and now we were living the reality of being called to be a full-fledged licensed minister of the gospel.

The Antioch church did invite me to serve as their pastor, and we gladly accepted. Antioch was a big church, compared to Weaverville.

MY BIOLOGICAL MOTHER

Many of the people who worked in the conference office worshiped there, as did many other professional people. It was definitely going to be a challenge—I would learn to depend on the Lord more than ever before. This church had not had an evangelistic series in ten years, and the Lord was moving on my heart to conduct one.

After several months of planning and heart-searching, our first evangelistic series was a blessing of magnificent proportions. A number of new members joined the church, and many older members rediscovered the joy of evangelism.

Leaving Weaverville had been a bittersweet experience. It was hard to leave the church family we had grown to love so much. But it meant leaving my mother, as well. She wanted to move to Antioch with us, but I told her we needed some space to get ourselves established. I said, "Mom, you are demanding that I love you as a son should naturally love his mother. But I need time to allow that kind of love to grow. I love you for giving me life, but sometimes I feel that our connection is just biological."

You would have thought I had said a bad word. "So I'm just your biological mother?" she cried. "Is that what you feel about me?" I did not mean it the way she made it sound. I was just asking her for time and space to grow into a "mother and son" relationship.

After we moved, I kept in touch with her regularly. But one day I couldn't reach her, and when I investigated further, I found that she had moved out of town and had not left a forwarding address. I wrote her expecting to get a letter back, but there was no response.

Around Christmas the next year, we received a card from her, but there was no return address. She signed the card, "Your Biological Mother!"

I had heard that my mom was good at cutting off people when she was upset. Her sister Teresa had told me about receiving similar cards when my mother lived in New York. We did not hear from her again until the next Easter. The phone rang, and a very cheerful voice said, "Hi, John, this is your mom, Rosie!" She said it as though we had never lost contact.

"Mom, what happened?" I almost shouted. "Where have you been, and why haven't you called me?"

She had a simple answer, "You said you needed space, so I was giving you space!" Before I could respond, she said, "Are you going to come to see me?" Mom was in control of the conversation, and she was not giving me the upper hand. She said, "I'm in Pleasanton, California. I sure would like to see you and Angie."

When we arrived at her house, I asked, "Mom, how long have you been in Pleasanton? How did you find this job?"

She said to me, "You don't know your mother very well. When I put my mind to doing something, I get it done!"

I couldn't question that. I was seeing what made her a survivor. I also began to understand my own emotional determination and drive. Both my mother and father possessed the determination to make their dreams happen. They were never at a loss for words. They never got lost in a crowded room—neither one was shy.

Mom liked taking photographs. I said, "Mom, you and Val are just alike. I see that her love for pictures comes from you." It was amazing to see how much Val and I were like our mother, considering that we had never lived with her. I did not realize how strong heredity was until I began to see it play out in my life and my sister's life.

There was much to talk about as we caught up on the happenings in each other's lives. At one point in our conversation, my mother smiled at me and said, "You need to listen to your biological mother!" We laughed it off. Then we apologized to each other for overreacting.

"Mom," I said, "I did not mean that you are 'just my biological mother.' I truly love you!"

She pushed her chair closer to me, embraced my arm, leaned on my shoulder, and said, "Remember, you are not 'just my biological son' either. I love you also!"

While we were visiting, I noticed that she kept rubbing her upper back. "Mom, did you strain your back lifting your patient?"

She thought so. I found out she had already had X-rays and had an MRI scheduled. "I'll let you know what the outcome is," she promised.

She did. Her phone call came from the hospital. "The doctor wants me to stay overnight. And he wants to speak to someone in my family, and that means you."

Many thoughts tumbled through my mind as Angie and I drove to the hospital. When we arrived, Mom seemed to be her cheerful self. But I did see a glimmer of concern in her eyes. "What's the latest?" I asked.

"The doctor said something about cancer," she answered. "He didn't say how bad it was or what kind it was. You know how doctors are!" All I could do was hug her.

She didn't seem stressed. She asked Angie to take a photo of the two of us. Just as the camera flashed, the doctor walked into the room. "Hi, Maria!" he said. Mom liked to be called Maria. "Are these your children?"

Mom introduced us, and then he said, "Come with me. I would like to show you the MRI scans that we did on Maria."

Mom looked at us and said, "I'll be here when you get back; go ahead." With a smile on her face, she gave us a backhand wave as if to urge us on to go with the doctor.

The doctor walked slowly toward his office as we talked. "I'm glad you came here, because your mom needs someone to be with her. I talked with her about what showed up on the scan, but I wanted to have you here so I could give you the full picture."

"What do you mean 'the full picture'?" I asked. "Is there something you didn't tell her? How bad is it?"

He pointed to an orange and reddish mass above the heart, on her MRI. "That's a cancerous tumor. Tests show that it is an aggressive form of cancer called 'small cell carcinoma.' She needs to begin a six-month chemotherapy program fairly soon."

I had to ask for the bottom line. "Doctor, what do you mean by 'an aggressive form of cancer'?"

"Well, let me just put it this way," he said quietly. "Make the next six months of her life the best times you've ever had. Spend time with her and reminisce about the past. Make her comfortable."

I looked at Angie. She immediately insisted, "Your mother needs to move in with us. I'm going to tell her to come with us to Antioch."

After she left, I asked the doctor if there was any hope of the cancer being removed. "Because of its size, it's too delicate to remove from that spot. But if it shrinks to a safe size after the six months of treatment, then we can consider the next step."

The next day, Mom moved into our home. She said, "John, see how hard it is to get rid of me!" We had to laugh.

Angie told her, "Make yourself completely at home. Whatever you need, just let us know. We want you to get your rest." But Mom looked the picture of health. I could not remember a time when she looked better than she did that evening. There was no external sign of her inward condition. And if we were waiting for her to get sad and depressed, we were waiting on the wrong person.

As soon as Mom got her chemotherapy-treatment schedule, she set her mind to battle her cancer. She insisted on driving herself to the hospital for her treatments. And she carried on with life as if nothing was wrong. Instead of becoming ill, her appetite increased. After about the second month, her lovely hair began to fall out. Her response? "John, I need to buy me a wig." A week later, she asked me to cut off the rest of her hair! I have to admit, without her hair—and with our family ears—she looked like Yoda from *Star Wars!*

The tension that Mom and I struggled with in Weaverville was non-existent. She and I had the time of our lives. She went to church with us and stayed pretty active. She did begin to tire more easily. One evening she asked me a favor. "John, the family really doesn't know me for who I have become. What I mean is, they were not here to see my baptism. They don't understand the changes the Lord has made in my life. Even if I told them, it would be hard for them to remember me as anyone but the Rosie they knew for so many years." With tears welling up in her eyes, she continued, "John, if anything happens to me, I want you to tell the family about the changes that took place in my life after I found the Lord. I want you to tell them about the truth I found. Don't forget to let them know I never went back to smoking and drinking."

"Mom," I said, "I promise that you can count on me to do that for you. I hope you know it's not going to be easy for me if you die. But I also know that the Lord will be able to give me strength if I need it."

I had to ask why she felt the urgency to ask that of me. She said, "I know that the doctor said it is an aggressive cancer. And just in case the treatments don't help, I didn't want you to have to think about what I would have wanted you to say."

Later she said, "I would like to see my sister Teresa. But the doctor won't allow me to travel until all the treatments are done." So she continued her treatments with that hope in mind. What none of us knew was that her sister was already planning to come and visit her.

Aunt Teresa surprised us all and brought a fresh burst of happiness to Mom. While she was there, it occurred to me that I might get better answers to some of my questions if I could ask them while Aunt Teresa and Mom were there together. I suggested we make a videotape of a question-and-answer session. Mom really liked the idea of making a tape, so we set up the camera and sat on the couch together. In the next several hours, I learned a lot about my family, my mother, and my past.*

Six months came and went quickly. Mom weakened near the end of the treatments, but she remained determined to travel to Florida to see Teresa again. They were really very close, even when they seemed to be at odds. After careful consideration, the doctor gave her good news. "Maria, your tumor has shrunk considerably. In light of that, I can clear you for travel. However, when you get to Florida, I want you to keep seeing a doctor for treatment of your cancer."

Mom didn't hesitate. We booked a flight, and she headed happily across the country again.

---

* I've included a transcript of the tape in the Appendix for those who might be interested.

CHAPTER THIRTEEN

Not Enough Time

When Mom got to Orlando, everything started off great. She was happy, and as she kept in touch regularly, the future seemed brighter than it had in a long time.

But about two weeks later, Teresa called. "John, your mother is in a clinic in Eatonville, Florida. Her cancer has metastasized to her brain. I took her to Florida Hospital, but they turned her away, because she did not have health insurance." I listened as she explained that the clinic was not equipped to help her. "What should I do?" she cried.

I was angry and sad at the same time. I felt helpless being on the other side of the continent. The most immediate thing I could do was pray. After I prayed, the Lord impressed me to call Max Mace. I remembered meeting his nephew, Rick, a few years before, and I remembered that he was an administrator at Florida Hospital. Max gave me Rick's number, and when I called, he remembered me.

He was nearly as angry as I was to hear what had happened with my mother. He said, "John, I'm having an ambulance sent to the Eatonville clinic to bring your mother here. I will personally wait for her arrival. Don't worry; I'll see that your mother is taken care of. Any friend of my uncle Max is a friend of mine."

A few hours later, he called to inform me that my mother had been admitted and given a private room. He also told me to ask my aunt Teresa to come see him. Rick told Teresa not to worry about the costs—they would be taken care of.

Even now, as I write this, tears come to my eyes thinking of how good God is to me. He touched Rick's heart at a time when we needed help and hope. I thank the Lord, and I want to acknowledge my endless gratitude to the Mace family, to Max and Rick. Thanks from our hearts.

At that time, I couldn't afford to fly to Florida, so I went to get new tires on my car for the long drive. I was standing outside the tire shop when I heard a voice, "John! Pastor John!" It was one of my members, Donna Church. She told me that Dr. Gene had been looking for me and that our airline tickets were already paid for. That news was another way the Lord was telling us "Don't worry, I will carry you through this!"

I hurried to the medical park where Dr. Gene Zimmerman and his wife, Esther, had their practice, along with the other doctors who attended our church. His son Dan was there, along with another church member, Dr. J. L. Edwards. I discovered that they had pooled funds to make it possible for Angie and me to fly to Florida. We were so grateful for their kindness that when we returned, Angie and I hosted a dinner at our home as a way of showing our appreciation. Thanks again, my friends.

When we arrived at the Florida Hospital in Orlando, I was taken aback by what I saw. My mother was in a semisedated state. She was conscious of her surroundings, but she would slip in and out of coherence.

But there was an uplifting side to the visit. It was at my mother's bedside in the hospital that I met my brother James (Jimmy) for the first time. He and I were like two kids in a candy store. I must say that, at first, it was somewhat awkward to meet my brother for the first time, more than thirty years after I was born. We said Hello and then started talking as if we had known each other all of our lives. I was taller, his hair was longer, and both of us were competitive and outgoing. He had a very strong West Indian accent.

I also met my mother's other sisters for the first time—Gloria, Julie, and Eneida. The only one I was yet to meet was Virginia. How ironic it was that in life, my mother kept us apart, but now that her life was slipping away, she was able to bring us together. I must say I was so pleased the Lord was giving me my natural family back. Most of the family I grew up with in New York was my surrogate family. The Lord provided the family unit I needed at the time I needed it.

That evening we went to Aunt Teresa's and became better acquainted. My sister was also there. Our aunts kept telling Val she looked just like her mother. Whenever she walked into a room, someone said, "She looks just like Rosie did when she was younger!" Val and I were welcomed into the family with open arms. It was as if we had known them all our lives. After a lengthy weekend of family acquaintances and re-acquaintances, Angie and I returned to California.

I kept in touch with Aunt Teresa about Mom's condition. Two weeks later, Mom passed away. When I heard, I began to cry profusely and then suddenly stopped. My emotions collided as if I was reliving 1984 when I first met my mother. With helpless feelings, I said to Angie, "What am I going to do? I did not have enough time with my mother! We were just getting to know each other!"

The consolation I found at that painful moment was the blessing of knowing I have the hope of being reunited with my mother in the resurrection. My comfort and assurance began to build. I said, "Angie, I am so glad I had the privilege to baptize my mother. At least we have eternity to look forward to!"

My sister and I made arrangements to go to St. Thomas for our mother's funeral. We knew we would meet many, many family members and friends there for the first time. We were getting an opportunity to go to our "roots." So there was a real joy mixed in with our sadness. We were saying Farewell to our mother and Hello to our family.

Mom died on October 24, 1991, and the funeral was six days later. She lived just fifty-eight years. The service was held in the crowded John Thomas Memorial Chapel in downtown St. Thomas. I stood looking into the faces of my family. My brother, Jimmy, my sister, Vivian, and I were brought together by a common bond, love for our mother.

When the service began, I remembered to do as my mother requested. I prayed and asked the Lord to give me the strength to make it through the service. Immediately the Lord shielded my emotions, and I was able to share with my family how Val and I were raised without their knowledge. I shared the circumstances of meeting Mom in 1984. Then I ended by telling the glorious story of the Lord coming into Mom's life and my joy at baptizing her. Just as my mother requested, I told the family about the truth she had accepted and about the progress and changes that the Lord gave her the strength to accomplish.

As I finished, I sang the song I dedicated to Mom when I met her—"My Treasure." As soon as I was done, I walked into the foyer of the funeral chapel, sat down on the bench, and succumbed to a flood of tears. My brother and sister joined me, and together we cried.

The burial was not far from the funeral home. In keeping with the traditions of the island, a funeral train was formed as everyone walked from the funeral home to the gravesite. The only car in the train was the one that carried the coffin. The song that was playing on the outside speakers of the vehicle was "Amazing Grace." When sadness comes and heartache spills over into the experience of life, that song reminds us that the only hope we have is the amazing grace of the Lord.

We stayed at the grave until it was covered and encased in a partially above-ground crypt. Jimmy, Val, and I each took flowers from the grave to form a memorial for Mom. To this day, I have the flowers, the funeral program, and the newspaper article of the passing of Rosario Maria Lomacang.

While at the cemetery, I learned more of the history of the family. When settlers from France came to St. Thomas, they built what is now called "French Town." Many of the residents of French Town are my family members. I gained a deep appreciation for my ethnicity. On my mother's side, I am French and Filipino. On my father's side, I am African American and American Indian. My family is a rainbow of races and cultures. From white skin and blue eyes to brown skin and black eyes, the cultures merge. French and Spanish, West Indian and Filipino were all represented in our St. Thomas family.

I had even found a connection to my grandfather's family. One of my Antioch church members, Edwin Villarosa, knew a Lomacang family in the Philippines. He brought back pictures, and there was a strong family resemblance—especially in the face and ears. I hope someday to take a trip back there myself to meet that side of the family.

My sister and I stayed at our aunt Gloria's home and continued our visit with family. That evening, my brother's wife, Ann, asked about the message I shared at the funeral service. "How could we get more information about the Bible and the things that Rosie believed?"

"When I get back to California, I will send you some materials."

She was serious. "That's not soon enough. Here is my Federal Express account number. When you get back, please send as much as you can, as quickly as you can."

When I returned to California, I sent a box of Bibles, lessons, Revelation Seminar materials, and pamphlets weighing 38.5 pounds by second-day Federal Express. I was so excited that they had a real interest in the message and truth of the Bible.

It had taken the Lord seven years to perfect His plan for my mother's life. Her life was complete in Jesus. She rested in the complete assurance of the resurrection. My sister and I realized the blessing of knowing our mother before she passed. Out of all that we could have asked for, the Lord went well beyond our expectations.

My great desire is that my family also gets to know the truth that "Rosie" came to understand and accept. I ask that you keep them in your prayers. The only thing that would make heaven even more glorious than it is going to be would be having all my family there. It is my deepest desire to see that prayer answered. I spent only one Christmas, one birthday, one Mother's Day, and one Easter with my mother, but I am looking forward to making up for lost time in the world made new.

CHAPTER FOURTEEN

Precious Papa

The Antioch church was our first big church. There were many bright experiences, but there was also much turbulence along the way. My personal life was often in crisis during our tenure there. My mother passed away in 1991. Then Angie and I had the responsibility of raising two nieces. In 1994, the situation with Papa Haynes grew more and more critical.

One of my greatest desires was to move Papa to California to live with Angie and me. He was getting older, and living downstairs at Madison Street was getting progressively more difficult. When I called, he would make it appear that things were "under control." But knowing Papa as well as I did, I knew he was just covering up the real nature of the situation. As often as possible, I went back to Brooklyn, New York, to spend time with him.

I always called him on holidays and birthdays, but in 1993, I spent Christmas in New York with him, while Angie was in Florida with her mother. I loved him so much that just being there with him was the best Christmas present he ever gave me. In light of all he had done for me, he had already given me the best present—himself.

While I was there, a cousin of Papa's came over with papers to sign, giving him power of attorney for Papa. It seemed like a good idea at the time, since this cousin was so much closer than I, and Val was so busy. Soon it would become clear how wrong we were.

That next year, Papa's health began to fail. In our phone conversations, he sounded weaker and weaker. Val lived in the house, but she had a very hectic schedule working as an EMT for New York. Papa sounded lonely. I went home in the early spring to check on him. When I arrived, I was horrified.

Obviously, the cousin who was responsible for Papa had slacked off on the job. I was so angry I couldn't sleep. I bought sixty dollars' worth of cleaning supplies and spent hours scrubbing floors and countertops. Before we went to bed that night, Papa said, "John, this is why I wish you were living here in New York instead of California." I told Papa I wanted to take him with me to California. For the first time, he was agreeable, but he wanted to get some things straight before he left.

I tucked Papa in bed and had prayer with him. When I left his room a few minutes later, I heard him mumbling in the dark. After a moment, I realized that he was praying! I was exhausted and still angry about the situation, but a light of hope came on in my heart. The next day Papa asked me about the church in California and how it was working out. That was an open door for me. I talked about his first wife, Carmen. I reminded him that Mama was resting in the grave, waiting for the coming of the Lord. I said, "Papa, nothing would make me more happy than to have you in heaven with us. When you come to California next year, I want to baptize you."

He did not disagree. He said in a soft voice, "That's possible."

I wanted to take Papa back with me when I left a few days later. But Val assured me she would hire a home attendant to take care of Papa during the day and someone to keep the house clean. With that arrangement, I felt he would be fine until we saw each other again.

I kept in touch, and for a while things went well. But then a conflict arose between him and his cousin over money. Before I knew it, his cousin had made plans to put Papa in a care facility in Barbados that would cost less. To make matters worse, he was planning to trick Papa into going by telling him it was just a family visit.

I called Papa to tell him about his cousin's plans. Papa was furious, and we planned for me to fly to Barbados and take him back with me to California. But because the cousin had power of attorney, he could make legal decisions for Papa, and his name was on Papa's property. I begged his cousin not to take Papa to Barbados before I had a chance to see him (and we could change the power of attorney). But he refused to wait. There was nothing I could do but say Goodbye to Papa and assure him I would come to Barbados to get him.

After Papa arrived in Barbados, he called Val and told her to hire a lawyer to get his cousin's name removed from the ownership papers of the house. Val hired the attorney and bought a ticket for Barbados. But the day before she left, Papa died.

We were crushed. Besides the sorrow we felt, there was a lot of anger and suspicion when the timing was so perfect to protect his cousin's interests in Papa's house and money. To make matters worse, Papa's cousin had arranged for burial in Barbados. "Didn't you know that he had a plot already paid for, right next to his first wife?" I shouted at him on the phone. With no help from the cousin, it took a month to make arrangements to bring Papa home to Brooklyn. It seemed clear to me that Papa's cousin was hiding something. I even contacted a private investigator, but it soon became clear that we could spend a fortune and still prove nothing. I had to let it go.

To make a long story short, the cousin was the executor of Papa's property, and it quickly become clear that he was manipulating the situation for personal gain and that he had been after Papa's money all along. It turned into a three-year legal battle with him over the property and its funds. Eventually, the court ruled in my favor, and the case was closed. But it took a tremendous toll on me and my ministry.

I had grown so full of hate for that man that I was losing my ability to function normally. It was getting difficult to read the Bible and preach.

Finally one evening, a book led me to look at the life Jesus led, and I realized I was losing the battle, because I was allowing my natural inclinations to lead me. I was not asking the Lord to remove my hatred and pain. I was seeking to settle the issue rather than take it to the Lord. When that truth hit me, I dropped the book and began to cry profusely. "What's wrong?" Angie asked with deep concern.

"Angie, God just showed me who I really am. I didn't know that I had been so consumed with hate. I did not even realize how far I had gone with letting this exist in my heart." She climbed out of the bed and held me to comfort me. We knelt together, and I asked the Lord to forgive me for letting Him down and for allowing myself to be swept away as I was.

That weekend, Elder Walter Pearson, a good friend of mine, was at an evangelism council being held in southern California. After one of the meetings, I shared with him about my struggle the past year. I asked him to pray for the Lord to take it from me. He talked with me, and then he prayed for me. For the first time in months, I came to the place where I was living in freedom. I had not only been made free, I embraced the walk and life of freedom. Our home was a more pleasant place, because my mind was not somewhere else. My sermons and ministry returned to a meaningful place, because the Lord strengthened me. From that day on, I have been free from any feelings of vengeance and hatred toward Papa's cousin.

It was not until after these events that I understood what the Lord was teaching me. When I was a young man, I was angry about my life, angry about being abandoned, and angry with my mother and father for leaving me. I was even angry with my father for coming back and not giving me the attention I needed. I had a strong temper when I was dating my girlfriend, who is now my wife. The Lord wanted to thoroughly cleanse me of my anger. He allowed me to be pushed to where the anger would come out so I would see I needed to be free.

Now I can speak firsthand to people about the issue of anger. I know how it can deaden our walk with the Lord. I know that it is like a cancer that can only be remedied by asking the Lord to take it, and then willingly releasing it so that He *can* take it. You see, freedom is not what we would eventually have; it is what we could have today, if we would only admit that we desperately need Christ. Now I can victoriously say, "I can do all things through Christ who strengthens me" (Philippians 4:13, NKJV).

CHAPTER FIFTEEN

Dreams Come True

Being ordained is the highest recognition the church can bestow on its ministers. And just eight years after I began as a "wet behind the ears" task-force worker with no degree in ministry, the conference voted to ordain me as a gospel minister. I felt like the apostles in the New Testament. Others considered them "ignorant and unlearned," but being with Jesus had made them the most effective ministers.

As the date set for our ordination drew near—I believe the Lord places His blessing not just on the pastor but also on the pastor's wife—we rejoiced that so many of our friends and family would be present. Then, out of the blue, the Internal Revenue Service contacted the conference with serious accusations about our tax reports. The conference decided to delay the ordination until that matter was resolved.

I was devastated, since I knew the IRS charges were incorrect. Angie and I took time away that weekend to focus on our relationship with God and His mission for our lives. Then on Monday morning, we contacted the IRS office to present our side of the issue. That afternoon, as a committee met at the conference office to discuss my fate, the IRS faxed an apology acknowledging that it was their error. A same-day response from the IRS admitting error? That's what I call God in action! The conference voted to go on with my ordination service as planned.

For the service, the church was full to capacity with members from all the churches I had served as pastor, as well as friends and family. The only sad moments in the celebration were in memory of those who were missing—my mother, my father, and Papa and Momma Haynes, without whom I would not have been where I was.

Five years had come and gone for us at Antioch. Now more than ever, I was determined to work in evangelism full time. I interviewed with the Amazing Facts organization, where Doug Batchelor had recently been named director/speaker. He encouraged me to join him. Amazing Facts was in the process of moving to California, and I planned to join them as soon as they were settled.

During the waiting time, I was encouraged to interview with the Fairfield church, which was looking for a pastor. When I explained my plans to go into evangelism rather than pastoring, the conference president said, "John, you already have a church. You can always say No if Fairfield invites you to join them."

I went to the interview and asked as many tough questions as I could. But the answers were always favorable. The members were friendly. The atmosphere was warm. The interview went well. Afterward, Angie asked, "How did you feel about the interview? Do you want to go to Fairfield?"

"You know I don't want to pastor another church," I said. "Whether they vote favorably or not, I still don't want to go to Fairfield!"

What Angie said next opened my eyes. "John, you sound like you did when we lived in Orlando. Remember that you told the Lord you were willing to go anywhere except California? Well, California is where He wanted you to be. What if He wants you to go to Fairfield? Are you going to tell Him No again?"

And I realized that she was right. I needed to keep my heart open to the leading of the Lord. We decided to ask the Lord for a sign. "If the

Lord wants us to go to Fairfield, He'll close the doors to evangelism with Amazing Facts."

Right away we received word that Fairfield had voted to ask us to join them. But I couldn't respond until I got a sign from God about evangelism. Within days, Doug called. "John, Amazing Facts is running into difficulties. It may be a year before we can find the right place to move to in California."

We accepted the invitation to Fairfield. And before long, the Lord opened the door for me to participate in evangelism at the New York '99 Millennium of Prophecy meetings with Doug Batchelor. This opportunity brought up another issue. For years people had asked if my songs were available on a CD. With a national audience planned for the New York meetings, the time seemed right to pursue that dream. I committed it to the Lord in prayer.

During this time, I was asked to organize a musical program for the Northern California Convocation. Karen Thomas, the wife of pastor Samuel Thomas, Jr., approached me afterward and asked, "John, do you have a CD?" When I answered No, she asked, "Why not?"

"I don't have the money!" I replied.

She shook that off. "If that's all that you need, that's not a problem. God could provide that!" Then she invited Angie and me to her home that evening.

Elder E. E. Cleveland, whom I had met just that day, was there also. He looked at me and repeated what he had told me earlier: "Young man, the Lord has an anointing on you!"

In the midst of our visit, Karen made a phone call. Before long, she said, "John, Adrian Westney, from the Breath of Life Quartet, wants to speak to you."

On the phone I learned that Karen had sold him on my music. He said, "Karen tells me that you want to make a CD, but you need sponsorship. I never do this with someone I don't know, but based on Karen's recommendation, I am committing myself to sponsoring a project for you."

After we saw how the Lord had provided the funding needed, Angie reminded me of a talk that she had with the Lord. She said, "Now I remember what He meant when He told me that nothing is impossible for Him."

I could hardly believe what I was hearing but sent him some songs immediately. Soon after I recorded "I Give All My Life to You," Adrian called again to say, "You're ready."

I got to work on the details of rights, permissions, and a photo for the cover, while I made arrangements to travel to Maryland for the recording session. When I arrived, I discovered that David Griffith, the brother of Bob Griffith, a former bass player for the Heritage Singers, was the sound engineer. Much to his surprise, we recorded all ten songs in two days. He said, "John, I have listened to many good artists, but you are one of those who really sings from the heart."

A few weeks after the New York series began, I had the finished CD in hand, and it was an instant hit. Once again the Lord poured His blessings on us. I thank the Lord for people like Samuel and Karen Thomas and Adrian Westney, who listen when the Lord impresses hearts to fulfill His will.

Final Words

As of the writing of this book, Angie and I have been in Fairfield for six years. We are leaving our future in the Lord's hands.

However, we are in quite a different world than we were before September 11, 2001. On that fateful day, Angie and I were on United Airlines 777 flying home from England when we heard about the tragic events in New York City, Washington, D.C., and Pennsylvania. Our flight was diverted to Canada, where we were detained for three days before being allowed to return to the U.S. As native New Yorkers, our hearts went out to our city and our fallen heroes. As a former worker in the World Trade Center, I thank the Lord that His plans removed me from harm's way long before the incident.

I solicit your prayers for my sister, Vivian Lomacang, who is an emergency medical technician for the Fire Department of New York City. She has been at "Ground Zero" each day working with a resolute spirit. Pray that through it all, she will respond to God's voice. Please keep my sister's daughter, Tiashia, in your prayers also.

I also ask that you remember my brother, James (Jimmy). He's been a professional fisherman in St. Thomas for years. It is my prayer that he, too, will see that the world is a fragile place and that only the eternal kingdom matters. I pray that my brother and I become the modern James and John and that we can be fishers of men for the Lord.

Please keep my father, John Parker, in your prayers also. As a jazz musician, he's been blowing his trumpet for over fifty years. My desire is that he plays it for the Lord in the earth made new.

We have learned to trust the Lord implicitly. As you have read this book, you may wonder why I use the word *Lord* so much. The answer is simple. Jesus is more than our Savior—He is our Lord. As our Savior, Jesus paid for our sins. But when we turned our lives over to Him, He became our Lord!

As Angie and I have moved from place to place, we have had many landlords. Every home we rent comes with a contract we must sign. One of the parameters of that contract is that we must remember we are accountable to the landlord for the property he entrusts to us.

In the same way, we are accountable to our heavenly Lord, the One who has entrusted the ministry to us. We are just stewards, and we pray to remain humble and faithful. To be forsaken by man does not mean to be forgotten by God. The Lord has promised that He will never leave us and never forsake us.

My life is a miracle, not because I learned to adjust, but because I am part of a Divine plan. I am moving upward and onward, not because I have learned to scale the utmost heights, but because I know Whose I am: I am a child of the King.

I choose not to fear life but to live it. I look back not to lament but to remember. I hold on not because I am incapable, but because I am wise. I look at barriers as movable, problems as solvable, heartache as healable, and disappointment as temporary. It is not confidence in myself that gives me hope; it is Christ in me that *is* my hope. The experiences I've had were not designed to break me but to make me. I am at peace because I know who I am.

If, in the midst of your circumstances you can see God, you are on your way to wholeness. If in the midst of your storms you can hear His voice, you are on your way to peace. To be abandoned is out of your control, but to think that you are alone is your choice.

Keep Angie and me in your prayers that we remain faithful to God's plan.

My Anchor Texts
- Psalm 27:10 (NKJV): "When my father and my mother forsake me, then the LORD will take care of me."
- Hebrews 13:5, 6 (NKJV): "Let your conduct be without covetousness; be content with such things as you have. For He Himself has said, 'I will never leave you nor forsake you.' So we may boldly say: 'The LORD is my helper; I will not fear. What can man do to me?' "
- Jeremiah 29:11 (NKJV): "I know the thoughts that I think toward you, says the LORD, thoughts of peace and not of evil, to give you a future and a hope."

APPENDIX

Interview With My Mother and Aunt Teresa

    I asked Mom and Aunt Teresa to sit on the couch, so I could videotape the entire conversation. I sat between them and asked the questions. There were times when Mom tried to evade answering, but her sister kept her on track. Sometimes Mom gave an answer she felt comfortable with, and her sister said, "Rosie, you need to tell the truth!" They disagreed with each other passionately, yet the answers kept coming. The two hours of conversation allowed me to see into my mom's past in a way I knew would have been impossible had not her sister been there.

    This is a glimpse into that conversation. Obviously, it is not convenient to give all the details that came up, so I will include only those things that I think are pertinent to the story.

    Question: Tell me about my heritage. How did my grandfather get to the Virgin Islands? Also, tell me the circumstances surrounding his death.

    Answer: Aunt Teresa said, "Your grandfather, Filicicimo Combis, was a steward on a merchant marine ship. His ship was traveling back from Germany on its way to the Philippines when he became ill. They

INTERVIEW WITH MY MOTHER AND AUNT TERESA

had to leave him at the hospital in St. Thomas for three months. By the time the next ship came through, my grandfather decided that he was not interested to go back to the Philippines, because he and his nurse, your grandmother, had fallen in love."

They married in 1929. The villagers' first response to their marriage was displeasure, because my grandfather was a foreigner. Aunt Teresa was born in 1931, and Mom was born in 1933. My grandfather spoke seven languages fluently, including many dialects from the Philippines and also Chinese. This was due to his extensive travel to different parts of the world.

When he decided not to go back to the Philippines, he decided to begin a fishing business. A boat was sent to him from the Philippines, a bigger boat than the U.S. Coast Guard's. Apparently, he came from a wealthy family. He had intended to take Rosie and Teresa to visit the Philippines, but by the time they made plans to go, Pearl Harbor was bombed, and travel to that part of the world ceased. There were three Filipino families in St. Thomas in those days: the Santos, Roldang, and Lomacang families.

Aunt Teresa went on to tell the story of my grandfather's disappearance. If you remember earlier in the book, Teresa told me that she was looking for someone who had the same name I had, because she was still hoping to find her father.

Her father and his friend, Oscar, were fishing on the large boat that my grandfather owned. It was during the time of prohibition, when there was a ban on selling illegal alcohol. Some of the islanders bootlegged alcohol between the islands by boat. He and his friend came upon a bootlegger's boat out of St. Barth's. Apparently, they asked for a split of the illegal money as the price of keeping quiet. But the men on the other boat disagreed and rammed his boat, throwing my grandfather and Oscar into the water. There one of them was beaten with an oar and the other was shot.

One of the sailors in the boat later confessed to a Catholic priest that they had killed two men at sea. The news was confidential, and, therefore, the priest kept it to himself for years. However, he shared it one evening when he went to a bar to get a drink.

Since Felicicimo was missing for so long, his wife, Inger, was living with another man—Andre. Another priest in town told them that they needed to get married. He also said that she could not marry unless it was proven that her husband was dead. The priest did his research and came back with the report that my grandfather, indeed, was killed at sea. Following that news, Inger married Andre.

Later, Teresa was offered a job teaching English on St. Barth's, and she accepted the assignment with the ulterior motive of finding the man who had killed her father. However, just before she left to go to St. Barth's, she learned that the man who had shot her father was dead.

In spite of the confirmation of her father's death, in the back of her mind, she hoped that it was not true. It would have been possible for him to leave St. Thomas and make it to Miami in his big boat. When she called the radio station looking for me in 1984, she was still driven by the hope of finding her father or his family.

Question: Could you explain what the proper spelling of my last name is?

Answer: This was much controversy over whether or not the name "Lomacang" had a tilde over the letter "a" or "n." My aunt contended that the name looked like this: "Lomacañg," with a tilde over the *n*. She said the Filipino culture adds it there. On the other hand, my mother contended that it is spelled "Lomacãng," with the tilde over the *a*. Teresa said that the ã is Spanish, and the ñ is Filipino. It amazed me that you could go from one culture to the other just by where the tilde was put in the name. They did agree that my grandfather's first name was Felicicimo. Mom said that it means "the most happy."

Question: Why was Jimmy, my brother, not with you in New York when you were planning to marry Jim Miller?

Answer: Mom claimed that when she met Jim Miller, the man I talked about in the early chapters, they planned to get married. She went to St. Thomas to get her oldest son, Jimmy, but her mother and

INTERVIEW WITH MY MOTHER AND AUNT TERESA

Andre hid Jimmy at someone else's house so that she would not be able to take him to New York. My mother said that her mother and Andre never told Jimmy the truth about the day they hid him and prevented her from taking him back to New York. Instead, they told him his mother abandoned him.

Mom concluded by saying, "That's why he hates me to this day. They never told him the truth. They told him I walked away from him. They also told him I was his sister." She also pointed out that in 1961, when she went to St. Thomas, Jimmy looked at her and said, "You're not my sister." Then she replied to him, "You're right, I'm your mother!"

Question: Mom, how long did you stay in St. Thomas when you went back in 1964 for your mother's funeral?

Answer: "I got a job and stayed there for two years, until I had a nervous breakdown in 1966." She said she talked with Jim Miller in New York, and he wanted to know if she was going to come back. She said she was not going to return until she had her son with her. However, she did return to New York for one week and then came back to St. Thomas to make another attempt at getting her son. The reason she gave was, "I did not like what was happening on this island." She said that Jim Miller finally broke up with her because he got tired of waiting.

Question: How much longer did you stay in St. Thomas? What was your condition when you were living in Orlando?

Answer: "I stayed there until 1970, and then I went to Orlando, Florida, to live with Teresa. During that time, I was in and out of mental hospitals. I also worked at the Orlando airport until 1976." She said, "It was like I was living in my body and watching someone else control it. In 1986, a minister told me that I had twelve or thirteen demons living in me." Concerning 1984 when we first met, she said, "When you guys met me, I was not myself."

Comment: When my mother made that comment, I realized that the Lord had delivered her from quite a spiritual bondage. That's why, when Angie and I picked her up in 1989 in California, she looked so different. She did not look like the same person I had seen when I met her in 1984. The Lord had freed her from years of demon possession and was preparing her for accepting Him into her life.

Question: When did you go back to New York to look for Val and me after you left us in 1958?
Answer: Mom said, "I went back in 1964 after my mother died. It was the same one-week period that I went back after I was not able to get Jimmy—in July of 1964."
Teresa commented: "In 1964, I didn't hear anything about John and Val."

Question: Where did the idea come from that Val and I died in a fire in New Jersey?
Answer: Teresa and Rosie agreed that the lady who first said that we had died in New Jersey was named "Maria Serano." This was a lady that Mom knew from St. Thomas. This lady had helped my mom when she was pregnant with her first child. Mom appealed to Maria to tell the truth about what I was doing in New York. Teresa said, "If I hadn't believed Maria Serano, I would have gone to New York to look for you and Val. Later I asked Rosie or Maria Serano how it happened, and one of them said, 'Your mother went to the store to buy milk, and when she came back, the house was on fire, and she could not get in to the children.'"

Question: When did you find out that you were pregnant with me?
Answer: Mom replied, "I was very ill when I was pregnant with you. I didn't even know that I was pregnant. I was about eighty-four pounds, and the doctor admitted me into the hospital for seventeen days. During that time, they gave me nourishment and vitamins. When I was healthy enough, they decided to give me one more exam. The doctors told me that I had a cyst, and they wanted to see what it was. When they made a small incision, they found out that I was pregnant, and they sewed me up and left you there." At the time, she was four

INTERVIEW WITH MY MOTHER AND AUNT TERESA

months pregnant. "When you were born, Momma Haynes refused to allow me to take you out much, because she said that you were too ill."

Question: Was I premature when I was born?
Answer: "No, you were full term, but I smoked and drank when I was pregnant with you."

Question: I heard that Val was missing when she was young. Tell us about that.
Answer: "Val was missing from the time that she was six weeks old until she was two years old. The people that were her baby sitters kidnapped her. The FBI searched for her for two years. That's why I had such a turbulent life living in New York. She was found in New Jersey. When Val was returned to me, anyone that was around me had to call me Mom so that Val would learn to call me Mom. I was pregnant with you when Val was returned."

Question: How is it that you were not able to find out where Val and I were?
Answer: "In 1964, when the cab driver took me to the house, there was a "Sold" sign on the building. I told the cab driver to drop me off at 15 Madison Street. I had a hard time dealing with losing you and Val again."

Question: Did you go to the police to ask for help to find us?
Answer: "No, I did not, because the police had found Val when she was kidnapped, and I didn't want them to think that I was a terrible mother."
Teresa commented: "While I was in St. Thomas, I tried to find out something about you two. When I heard that you and Val had died in New Jersey, I had no reason to go to New York. I did not know anyone in New York. I had heard of John Parker, but that was it. Rosie did not tell me about anyone else. I didn't know where John Parker lived, I didn't know what he did, and I didn't hear about any baby sitters."

Mom commented: "I did not want anyone in St. Thomas to know about John and Val, because I was afraid that they would try to take them from me as they took Jimmy."

Question: After you left New York, when you could not find us, did it dawn on you to look again after a little time passed? Did you know the phone number to call?

Answer: "When I went back to St. Thomas, I called three or four times and got no answer. Before I left New York, I went to Madison Street during the night. I thought for sure someone would be there. I just thought that something was wrong at the house, and when I called, I thought that something was wrong with the phone."

I commented: As I listened to my mother explaining her actions in 1964, I sensed that she was trying to dodge the real issue and make it appear that she did all she could. I had to interrupt and let her know how I felt. I said, "Mom, if I were you, I would have gone back to the house again. I would have thought that I was the one to make the mistake and that maybe I went to the wrong house. How could you just walk away and not make an attempt to find us? Did you think that calling the police for assistance in finding your children was an inconvenience to them or an inconvenience to you? From the perspective of your children, it is more difficult to think that you did all that you could to find us when Mr. and Mrs. Haynes never moved. Mom, let me summarize it this way: I feel that you may have had your life under your control and just the way you wanted it. I feel that you didn't want the responsibility of raising me and Val and that not coming back was not an accident."

Mom commented: "It was not so. I had to run away from your father. He and I were not going to stay together, and to try to run from him with you and your sister with me was something that I could not do. You should be glad that you were not raised by me!"

I commented: "I can accept the fact that things were rough for you, but as time went on, you should have contacted us and let us know

INTERVIEW WITH MY MOTHER AND AUNT TERESA

where you were, even if you said that you could not raise us. You owed it to us to let us know who and where you were."

Mom commented: "After I did not find you and Val in 1964, I just gave up on life. I frankly did not care about myself, and I did not care about you or Val or anyone else. After that event, I was blind to reality. I just gave up. John, I realize that you want to know the facts, but talking about it stifles me and makes me want to run away. That's how I handle it—I disappear until I want to talk about it. I had been criticized so often for my choices that I just felt like cutting everyone off."

Question: Why is it that I hear you putting the responsibility on anyone but yourself? Why is it so difficult to just say that Val and I fell victim to your desire to just cut us off?

Answer: "John, I understand how you feel, but I feel like a victim also. One thing after the other was backing up on me, and I just had to walk away from all of it to try to stay in my right mind. The problem was that walking away did not help me, and instead of coming after you and possibly messing up your life, I decided to leave it alone."

Question: Mom, you were in New York for six years after I was born. Why did you not come back during those years to get us?

Answer: "I was trying to get myself together. Where would I have put you? I did not have anything of my own. I was only living with whomever I was with. I was dodging your father, and it was not easy for me. I knew that you were fine with Mrs. Haynes, and I had no burden to mess up your life."

Question: Mom, how could you have been in the city for six years and not be able to get yourself together?

Answer: "Mrs. Haynes became very upset with me for not coming to visit you and Val. When I fell behind in paying her, she was upset. She wanted me to come over and sign you and Val over to her so that she could legally adopt you. I chose to not come back, because I was not going to sign you and Val over to her."

I commented: Mom, you mean to tell me that you allowed a lady who was literally just the baby sitter tell you that she wanted your children, and you did not challenge her?

Answer: "At the time, being alone and in conflict, it seemed like the right thing to do. So I just decided not to go back and argue with her. I look back, and I am glad that she raised you and Val. If I had, you would have never seen the inside of a church, much less become a minister!"

The Ending: The tape ran out after about two hours. It was about 11:00 p.m., and when the tape stopped, we continued talking for about another two hours.

Were all of the answers correct to fact? Probably not! Did I get all of my questions answered? No, I did not! Did I think that any good was served by taping the session? Absolutely! My mother never admitted that she just did not have room for her children when she was young. She refused to admit that we were an inconvenience at the time when she wanted to enjoy her single life.

The one thing I did notice was that her past was filled with pain. Much of it was based on her choices, and some of it was based on circumstances in her home life. Both she and her sister agreed that growing up with a man that was not their natural father was not an easy thing to do. Mom said she could not stand the circumstances in her home from the time her mother remarried. Leaving home was something she wanted to do as soon as she got old enough to do so; and she did. Keeping us away from St. Thomas was something she resolved to do, and she did. To this day, my sister and I still have a lot of family we need to get to know.

That night left me so much to process. I only wish I had had a second two-hour videotape.

I have learned to change the things I can and accept the things I cannot change. Meeting my mother was the biggest answer to prayer I had in my life. I consider myself very fortunate to have gotten an opportunity that many children, no matter their age, are still hoping to experience. I learned to love my mother for who she had become.

INTERVIEW WITH MY MOTHER AND AUNT TERESA

Short Biography of John Parker

John became known as "Tasty" Parker when New Orleans star drummer Zutty Singleton called him "Tasty" because of the tasty, improvised licks that come from Johnny's trumpet when he plays for delighted audiences worldwide!

Encouraged to play jazz trumpet by the great bassist George Duvivier, John graduated from high school in Flushing, Queens, then took his style to New York City's legendary clubs on Fifty-second Street. He played on the road with R&B bandleaders Roosevelt Sykes ("the Honeydripper") and Sax Kari. John recorded with Sykes, singer Etta Jones, Gatemouth Moore, Sy Oliver, and stepped in for Cat Anderson in Duke Ellington's band.

In the 1950s, Parker gigged with Sonny Rollins and Thelonious Monk and in the 1970s with pianist Brooks Kerr and famed drummer, Sonny Greer. "Tasty" Parker also played with Harry Connick, Jr. at the Algonquin Hotel and with Terri Thornton for the house jazz band at the Casa Bella Restaurant in Little Italy.

He is the quintessential New York City music personality, a "strolling trumpeter" who serenaded clients at the famous Chelsea Place. He appeared on the "Shining Star" video, which aired on Black Entertainment Television and other cable television stations.

Johnny Parker still plays his trumpet to audiences that gather weekly at Arthur's Tavern in downtown Manhattan. Among the comments you will hear is, "He's the best" and "I came here just to hear him blow his horn." After more than forty years of serenading, Johnny Parker's name still comes up whenever trumpet playing is discussed. He is truly one of a kind.

If you enjoyed this book, you'll enjoy these as well:

No More Broken Strings
Jaime Jorge. The intriguing story of the Cuban-born refugee who became a world-class violinist and music minister. Jaime writes honestly about his growth as a musician, his family and faith, as well as his mistakes and struggles with temptation.
0-8163-1905-7.

In His Hands
Sophie Berecz and Arpad Soo. The exciting true story of God's miraculous protection of a Romanian Adventist pastor who smuggled literature behind the iron curtain. Imprisonment, divorce, poverty and ultimately, financial blessings all play in part this amazing story.
0-8163-1903-0.

Mission Pilot
Eileen Lantry. The true adventures of David Gates, a missionary pilot who has repeatedly experienced the miracles of God in his life. Through hijackings, prison, and many other narrow escapes, David proves that living for God is still the highest adventure.
0-8163-1870-0.

Beyond the Veil of Darkness
Esmie Branner. A heart-pounding account of the struggles, hardships, and courageous triumph of a young Christian woman who refused to deny her faith in Christ despite the physical and mental abuse of a Muslim husband.
0-8163-1713-5.

Order from your ABC by calling **1-800-765-6955**, or get online and shop our virtual store at **www.adventistbookcenter.com**.
- Read a chapter from your favorite book
- Order online
- Sign up for email notices on new products

Prices subject to change without notice.